CliffsN

D0199027

Of Mice and Men

By Susan Van Kirk, M.Ed.

IN THIS BOOK

- Learn about the Life and Background of the Author
- Preview an Introduction to the Novel
- Study a graphical Character Map
- Explore themes and literary devices in the Critical Commentaries
- Examine in-depth Character Analyses
- Enhance your understanding of the work with Critical Essays
- Reinforce what you learn with CliffsNotes Review
- Find additional information to further your study in CliffsNotes Resource Center and online at www.cliffsnotes.com

Wiley Publishing, Inc.

About the Author
Susan Van Kirk has taught high school English for 31 years in Monmouth, Illinois.

Publisher's Acknowledgments

Editorial
Project Editor: Tracy Barr
Acquisitions Editor: Greg Tubach
Glossary Editors: The editors and staff at Webster's New World™ Dictionaries
Editorial Administrator: Michelle Hacker

Production
Indexer: York Production Services, Inc.
Proofreader: York Production Services, Inc.

Wiley Publishing, Inc., Indianapolis Composition Services

CliffsNotes™ *Of Mice and Men*

Published by:
Wiley Publishing, Inc.
909 Third Avenue
New York, NY 10022
www.wiley.com

Table of Contents

How to Use This Book

CliffsNotes *Of Mice and Men* supplements the original work, giving you background information about the author, an introduction to the novel, a graphical character map, critical commentaries, expanded glossaries, and a comprehensive index. CliffsNotes Review tests your comprehension of the original text and reinforces learning with questions and answers, practice projects, and more. For further information on John Steinbeck and *Of Mice and Men*, check out the CliffsNotes Resource Center.

CliffsNotes provides the following icons to highlight essential elements of particular interest:

Reveals the underlying themes in the work.

Helps you to more easily relate to or discover the depth of a character.

Uncovers elements such as setting, atmosphere, mystery, passion, violence, irony, symbolism, tragedy, foreshadowing, and satire.

Enables you to appreciate the nuances of words and phrases.

Don't Miss Our Web Site

Discover classic literature as well as modern-day treasures by visiting the CliffsNotes Web site at www.cliffsnotes.com. You can obtain a quick download of a CliffsNotes title, purchase a title in print form, browse our catalog, or view online samples.

You'll also find interactive tools that are fun and informative, links to interesting Web sites, tips, articles, and additional resources to help you, not only for literature, but for test prep, finance, careers, computers, and the Internet too. See you at www.cliffsnotes.com!

LIFE AND BACKGROUND OF THE AUTHOR

His Early Years

John Ernst Steinbeck, Jr., was born on February 27, 1902, in Salinas, California, to a father, John Ernst Steinbeck, who had settled in California shortly after the Civil War, and a mother, Olive Hamilton Steinbeck, who was a public schoolteacher. Steinbeck grew up in the beautiful, fertile Salinas Valley, and most of his memorable novels and short stories would be set in California. Situated between the Santa Lucia range and the Gabilan Mountains, this valley in west central California is bordered on the north by Monterey Bay and on the south by San Luis Obispo. During his early years, Steinbeck's mother read to him from books such as *Treasure Island* and *Robin Hood*. Young John grew up hearing the rhythms of the Bible and listening to the magical stories of the Round Table from Malory's *Le Morte d'Arthur*. He would return again and again to those early influences for symbols and themes.

During these early years, John's home was comfortable, and his father often drove the boy and his two sisters around the valley where they saw the workers and field hands in their poor shacks. This early impression of the workers' lifestyles was added to later memories when Steinbeck spent time with these workers as an adult. As a youngster, he also explored the caves and swimming holes around Salinas and watched the changes of seasons. His abiding love of nature and his thoughts about man's relationship to his environment are present in most of his works.

In high school, Steinbeck did well in English and edited the school yearbook. He worked at various jobs and one in particular—as a ranch hand on some of the local ranches—later led him to images used in *Of Mice and Men*. Steinbeck graduated from high school and went on to Stanford University. Even though he remained at Stanford until 1925, he never graduated. While in college, he continued to write creatively, and he worked for a time on neighboring farms, especially Spreckels Sugar Ranch. The agricultural industry at this time relied on cheap, transient labor. It was during this time that Steinbeck met many of the types of people described with compassion in his later writing.

His Early Career and Writing

Leaving Stanford, Steinbeck moved to New York and worked for five years at various jobs, writing and drifting. Eventually he returned to California, and his first book, *Cup of Gold*, appeared in 1929, two months before the stock market crash. This novel sold 1,500 copies, and its publication began a decade of recognition and material prosperity for Steinbeck.

In 1930, Steinbeck married Carol Henning whom he had met while working and writing at Lake Tahoe. He and Carol moved to Los Angeles, where Steinbeck continued his writing while Carol did a great deal of editing. Steinbeck also met marine biologist Ed Ricketts, who was a fascinating and talkative companion. Ricketts inspired the character for Doc in *Cannery Row* (1945) and many of Ricketts' views about biology influenced Steinbeck's literary themes. Ricketts later collaborated on the writing of *The Sea of Cortez: A Leisurely Journal of Travel and Research*, published in 1941.

During the decade of the 1930s—a time of national depression, bread lines, and bloody labor-management conflicts—Steinbeck knew a definitive cross-section of society and shared the problems and stresses of the times. In 1932, he received $400 dollars for the first of his California novels, *The Pastures of Heaven*. He followed this novel with *To a God Unknown* in 1933, but neither novel did well. During this difficult time, his mother suffered a stroke, adding to his discouragement. But also during this period, Steinbeck conceived the idea for *The Red Pony* and won the O. Henry Prize in 1934 for his story, "Murder." Two of Steinbeck's Pony stories were published in the *North American Review*, and he was beginning to enjoy some prominence. This was tempered in 1934, however, by the death of his mother.

Ironically, Steinbeck's breakthrough novel, *Tortilla Flat*, had garnered him five rejection slips by the time it was accepted in 1935 by New York publisher Pascal Covici. This book, about a group of California free spirits, called *paisanos*, has often been compared to the Arthurian stories because of the loyalty of its group of characters. The novel was an immediate popular success and won the Gold Medal of the Commonwealth Club of San Francisco as the year's best novel by a Californian. Just before its publication, however, Steinbeck's father died, missing the positive critical success of his son's writing. Steinbeck received $3,000 or $4,000 for the Hollywood film rights.

Encouraged, Steinbeck began his next project, a novel about a strike of agricultural workers organized by two communists. As predicted, this latest novel caused great fury because the labor movement at that time was causing distress to the large growers, who worried about strikes. Steinbeck titled the novel *In Dubious Battle* (1936), and it sold moderately well.

Of Mice and Men (1937), a popular and critical success, was selected by the Book-of-the-Month Club. Following its publication, Steinbeck toured England, Ireland, Russia, and Sweden. He returned to the United States and produced a play version of the book with famous playwright George Kaufman. The play won the New York Drama Critic Circle's Award on the first ballot and also became a popular film. When the play opened on Broadway, Steinbeck was already working on what most critics consider to be his masterpiece, *The Grapes of Wrath*.

The Grapes of Wrath came out of the time Steinbeck was working on *Of Mice and Men*, when he also accepted work writing for the *San Francisco News*. Steinbeck was assigned a story to cover migrant workers who swelled the California population at seasonal harvest times. Steinbeck decided to travel incognito and observe the living conditions and the violence of the migrant workers' lives. He published a series of articles in 1936 titled "The Harvest Gypsies." This experience moved his sense of compassion and stirred up his concern for social justice.

In preparation for writing a novel, Steinbeck went to Oklahoma, joined some migrants, and traveled with them to California. Once in California, he stayed with these migrants in "Hoovervilles," joining them in their search for work and observing firsthand their living conditions. A major publishing event of 1939, *The Grapes of Wrath* became a best seller and was the eighth ranking book of 1940 according to *Publishers' Weekly*. It was estimated that over half a million copies of the original printing were sold. The novel was translated into foreign editions and won an American Bookseller's award as well as the Pulitzer Prize for the best novel of the year. Steinbeck was also elected to membership in the National Institute of Arts and Letters. In a year of great motion pictures, the film version of *The Grapes of Wrath* competed with *Gone With the Wind* and *The Wizard of Oz*. The strong movie censorship of the times, however, took a lot of the bite out of Steinbeck's criticism of social injustices.

The Grapes of Wrath was not without its critics, however. The tough language and graphic scenes were too realistic to some readers, and others felt that Steinbeck showed too much sympathy for communist views. The California agricultural community, particularly the California growers and large landowners, were unhappy with Steinbeck's criticism of a system that bankrupted many of the small farmers who lost their land and became unhappy paid help for large growers.

Thrown increasingly into the public spotlight, Steinbeck experienced difficulties in his marriage. In an attempt to patch things up, he and Carol set off on a marine biology expedition with Ed Ricketts during the public controversy over *The Grapes of Wrath*. They traveled through the Gulf of California, later documented in *The Sea of Cortez*. But his marriage ended in divorce in 1943.

The War Years and Beyond

During the 1940s, Steinbeck did a great deal of traveling and writing. His interests turned to the rise of fascism, and he wrote a promotional book for the Army Air Force called *Bombs Away*. Steinbeck also wrote a World War II novella, *The Moon Is Down*, in which he described a small Norwegian village invaded and occupied by a thinly disguised Nazi force. The King of Norway decorated Steinbeck in recognition of his book's contribution to the liberation effort. Steinbeck also scripted a war movie called *Lifeboat* in an attempt to raise American morale. During this period, he married again to Gwen Conger with whom he had two sons. In 1943, while a correspondent for the New York *Herald Tribune*, Steinbeck wrote a collection of human interest articles later published in 1958 under the title *Once There Was a War*.

After the war ended, Steinbeck devoted himself to a number of writing projects that left the war behind. In 1945, he wrote *Cannery Row*, another well-received California book that followed the humorous adventures of the down and out, living in Monterey. *Cannery Row* was the first of two books in this period to be influenced by his friendship with the marine biologist, Ed Ricketts.

In 1947, Steinbeck wrote *The Pearl*, an allegory about a poor fisherman who finds a pearl that changes his life; Steinbeck's experiences from the trip to the Gulf of California back in 1940 provided the kernel of the story's plot. *The Pearl* was also filmed, as was another book published the same year and titled *The Wayward Bus*. Even though *The Wayward Bus* received poor reviews, it sold well and was a humorous story about a bus full of interesting Steinbeck characters. In 1948, Steinbeck received a blow with the death of Ed Ricketts in a car accident. His marriage to Gwen ended as well, and the divorce settlement brought grave financial difficulties. He returned once again to Pacific Grove to heal and to write.

His Last Two Decades

The 1950s brought a series of projects, including some novels, and a third and happier marriage. In 1950, Steinbeck married for the last time to Elaine Scott, the ex-wife of actor Randolph Scott. In the same year, he finished a screenplay for the film *Viva Zapata!* and published the novel/play *Burning Bright*, which was produced on Broadway. The following year, Steinbeck began work on a 600-page novel, *East of Eden*. *East of Eden* is similar to *Of Mice and Men* in that it revisits the biblical story of Cain and Abel. *East of Eden* is the tale of two families through several generations and is set in Salinas Valley. A story of good and evil, it was produced as a film in 1952 and later as a miniseries for television.

During this period, Steinbeck also revised *Cannery Row* and republished it under the title *Sweet Thursday* (1954). Rogers and Hammerstein later used his story for their musical *Pipe Dream*. Besides returning to his biblical themes, Steinbeck also returned to another childhood influence: the King Arthur stories. He began a book (that would be published posthumously) based on Sir Thomas Malory's *Le Morte d'Arthur*, renaming it *The Acts of King Arthur and His Noble Knights*. This book was rapidly followed in 1957 with *The Short Reign of Pippin IV*, a fantasy about medieval France but, like many of Steinbeck's later works, it received poor reviews.

By this time, several of Steinbeck's works had received poor critical appraisals, and he became discouraged and suffered what may have been a slight stroke. Still, during this time, he wrote *The Winter of Our Discontent*, which is set on the east coast and whose main character is the descendent of a Puritan heritage. Ethan Allen Hawley, the main character, sees the moral corruption that has become America. Deciding to join in the immorality, he finds—too late—that his son has been influenced by his example. Regarded as a criticism of middle class American values in modern society, the book was scorned by critics and readers alike who were not in the mood for Steinbeck's criticism. Characteristically, as it was being published, Steinbeck set off in a small truck with his black poodle, Charley, "in search of America."

That same year, 1961, Steinbeck was invited as a guest to attend the inauguration of President John F. Kennedy. The following year, the Swedish Academy awarded Steinbeck the Nobel Prize for Literature, the highest honor a writer can receive. The prize was presented for the body of his work, but it met with outcries from critics who felt Steinbeck had limited talent and was a writer of propaganda. Steinbeck took the opportunity in his acceptance speech to strike out at those critics, saying "Literature is not promulgated by a pale and emasculated critical priesthood, singing their litanies in empty churches. Nor is it a game for the cloistered elect, these tinhorn mendicants of low-caloric despair." Having received the Nobel Prize, however, was a mixed blessing: Although it gave Steinbeck a place of great honor in the literary world, it also put terrible pressure on his future writing.

Following Kennedy's assassination, Steinbeck became a friend of Lyndon Johnson. During the Viet Nam War, Steinbeck reported for *Newsday*, a Long Island newspaper, from the jungles of southeast Asia. His war dispatches were very militant, and he was deeply moved by the deaths of young American soldiers. (Both of his sons were in the army, and one was serving in Viet Nam.) Often a guest at the White House, Steinbeck supported American involvement in Viet Nam, and he lost friends who supported the anti-war movement. These years led to his last publications—testimonies to his thoughts and feelings about America.

Steinbeck's last two books were nonfiction. *Travels with Charley in Search of America* was an account of his trip from Maine to California. This journey was a pilgrimage of sorts in search of America, and he named his truck Rocinante, after the horse that carried the idealistic Don Quixote. Steinbeck's love for America is evident throughout this book, and he felt he had found the modern American character. His last book, *America and the Americans*, was about his faith that the country would come together despite the pains it suffered in the 1960s.

Steinbeck died on December 20, 1968, at his apartment in New York City. He was 66 years old. His wife took him home to Salinas, and he was buried not far from the many towns and ranches that sprang from his imagination and grace the pages of his books. A controversial writer during much of his life, Steinbeck is often remembered with the phrase used in the awarding of his Nobel Prize: ". . . he holds his position as an independent expounder of the truth with an unbiased instinct for what is genuinely American, be it good or bad."

INTRODUCTION TO THE NOVEL

Introduction

When John Steinbeck published *Of Mice and Men* in 1937, the world was in the grip of the Great Depression. Americans were out of work, breadlines were common day occurrences, and the future looked grim indeed. In California, there were economic and social problems that increasingly concerned Steinbeck and provided material for three novels about agricultural workers. By the time he wrote *Of Mice and Men*, the itinerant ranch hands were beginning to be replaced by machinery, and their way of life was fast disappearing. Nevertheless, Steinbeck's story captures the culture of those workers realistically and provides a vehicle for his thoughts about the common man.

Of Mice and Men is a dark tale, a parable of men journeying through a world of pitfalls and brutal, inhumane experiences. Their dreams seem all but doomed, obstacles block their ways, happiness appears to be an impossibility, and human handicaps affect their hopes. When the novel begins, we are treated to a forest scene with the sunshine on the pond and the gentle breeze in the willow trees promising that life is good. But soon after, that nature scene is replaced by a human world that contains jealousy, cruelty, loneliness, rootlessness, longing for land, and shattered dreams.

The power of John Steinbeck's vision is that we, the readers, enter this world and are drawn into the journey of these two men—Lennie and George—and we witness their dreams, their hopes, and their courage. Like so many of Steinbeck's characters, Lennie and George are not captains or kings but little guys. They haven't a dime to their names or a place to lay their heads, but they strive for a better life; they long for self respect, independence, freedom from fear, a future, a place to call home, and work that they love.

From the title—an allusion to Robert Burns' poem "To a Mouse On Turning Her Up in Her Nest with a Plow," November, 1785—however, we know that this journey will not be easy. First, Lennie and George have very few skills and resources that will help them attain their dreams. Second, their journey is made even more difficult because Lennie is mentally retarded; his powerful body, his childlike innocence, and his fascination with soft things conspire against him. Finally, Steinbeck fills their journey with obstacles, among them lack of family, cruelty and intimidation, jealousy, fear, loneliness, and self doubt.

What Lennie and George have going for them, though—what separates them from the other people they encounter and what makes the reader willing to take the journey with them—is that they have each other. As Lennie often says to George, "I got you to look after me, and you got me to look after you . . . ." In this way, they are not like the other ranch hands, who "are the loneliest guys in the world."

When John Steinbeck received the Nobel Prize for Literature, his acceptance speech avowed that ". . . the writer is delegated to declare and celebrate man's proven capacity for greatness of heart and spirit—for gallantry in defeat—for courage, compassion, and love." Lennie and George in *Of Mice and Men* embody these traits, which, according to Steinbeck, are the "bright rallying flags of hope and of emulation."

A Brief Synopsis

The novel opens with two men, George Milton and Lennie Small, walking to a nearby ranch where harvesting jobs are available. George, the smaller man, leads the way and makes the decisions for Lennie, a mentally handicapped giant. They stop at a stream for the evening, deciding to go to the ranch in the morning. Lennie, who loves to pet anything soft, has a dead mouse in his pocket. George takes the mouse away from Lennie and reminds him of the trouble Lennie got into in the last town they were in—he touched a girl's soft dress. George then reminds Lennie not to speak to anyone in the morning when they get to the ranch and cautions Lennie to return to this place by the river if anything bad happens at the ranch.

When he has to take the dead mouse away from Lennie a second time, George chafes at the hardship of taking care of Lennie. After calming his anger, George relents and promises Lennie they will try to find him a puppy; then he tells Lennie about their dream of having a little farm where they can be their own boss and nobody can tell them what to do, where Lennie will tend their rabbits, and where they will "live off the fatta the lan'." Lennie has heard this story so often he can repeat it by heart. And George emphasizes that this dream and their relationship make them different from other guys who don't have anyone or a place of their own. They settle down and sleep for the night.

The next morning at the ranch, the boss becomes suspicious when George answers all the questions and Lennie does not talk. George explains that Lennie is not bright but is a tremendous worker. They also meet Candy, an old swamper with a sheep dog; Crooks, the black stable hand; the boss' son Curley, who is an amateur boxer and has a bad temper; Curley's wife, who has a reputation as a "tart"; Carlson, another ranch hand; and Slim, the chief mule skinner. Upon seeing Curley's wife, Lennie is fascinated with her and George warns him to stay away from her and Curley.

That evening, Carlson complains bitterly about Candy's dog, which is old, arthritic, and smells. He offers to kill the dog for Candy, and Candy reluctantly agrees to let him do so. Later, after the others have gone to the barn, hoping to witness a fight between Slim and Curley over Curley's wife, Lennie and George are alone in the bunkhouse. Lennie wants to hear the story of their farm again, and George retells the dream. Candy overhears and convinces George and Lennie to let him in on the plan because he has money for a down payment. George excitedly believes that, with Candy's money, they can swing the payment for a ranch he knows of; he figures one more month of work will secure the rest of the money they need. He cautions Lennie and Candy not to tell anyone.

The ranch hands return, making fun of Curley for backing down to Slim. Curley is incensed and picks a fight with Lennie, brutally beating Lennie until George tells Lennie to fight back. Lennie smashes all the bones in Curley's hand. Taking Curley to a doctor, Slim gets Curley's promise to say his hand got caught in a machine so Lennie and George won't get fired. Lennie is afraid he has done "a bad thing" and that George won't let him tend the rabbits. But George explains that Lennie did not mean to hurt Curley and that he isn't in trouble.

Later that week, Lennie tells Crooks about the plans to buy a farm, and Crooks says he would like to join them and work for nothing. In the middle of their conversation, Curley's wife enters and, after Crooks tells her she isn't welcome in his room and that if she doesn't leave, he will ask the boss not to let her come to the barn anymore, she threatens him with lynching. Eventually, George returns and tells her to get lost. Dejectedly remembering his place, Crooks retracts his offer.

The next day, Lennie is in the barn with a dead puppy. While Lennie thinks about how he can explain the dead puppy to George, Curley's wife enters. They talk about how they enjoy touching soft things. She tells him he can touch her hair, but when Lennie strokes it too hard and messes it up, she gets angry. She tries to jerk her head away, and, in fear, Lennie hangs on to her hair. Curley's wife begins to scream. To keep her from screaming, Lennie holds her so tightly he breaks her neck. Knowing he has done something bad, he goes to the hiding place by the stream.

Candy finds the body of Curley's wife and goes for George; both men immediately know what has happened. Candy knows that Curley will organize a lynching party, and George says he is not going to let them hurt Lennie. George asks Candy to wait a few minutes before he calls the others; then he slips into the bunkhouse and steals Carlson's Luger. When Curley comes and sees his murdered wife, he vows to kill Lennie slowly and painfully. George joins the men searching for Lennie.

As they spread out, George alone goes straight for the riverside where he finds Lennie. Lennie knows he has done "a bad thing" and expects George to scold and lecture him. George, however, is so overcome with remorse that he cannot scold Lennie but must save him from Curley's cruelty. He tells Lennie to look across the river and imagine their little farm. George describes it, as he has done many times before, and while Lennie is smiling with pleasure and envisioning the rabbits he will tend, George shoots Lennie at the back of his neck. The others arrive, and George leads them to believe Lennie had Carlson's gun which George wrestled away from him and shot in self-defense. Only Slim comprehends the truth, and he takes George off up the footpath for a drink.

List of Characters

Lennie Small   A migrant worker who is mentally handicapped, large, and very strong. He depends on his friend George to give him advice and protect him in situations he does not understand. His enormous strength and his pleasure in petting soft animals are a dangerous combination. He shares the dream of owning a farm with George, but he does not understand the implications of that dream.

George Milton   A migrant worker who protects and cares for Lennie. George dreams of some day owning his own land, but he realizes the difficulty of making this dream come true. Lennie's friend, George gives the big man advice and tries to watch out for him, ultimately taking responsibility for not only his life but also his death.

Slim The the leader of the mule team whom everyone respects. Slim becomes an ally to George and helps protect Lennie when he gets in trouble with Curley. Slim has compassion and insight, and he understands George and Lennie's situation. He alone realizes, at the end of the novel, the reason for George's decision.

Candy Sometimes called "the swamper," he is a old handyman who lost his hand in a ranch accident and is kept on the payroll. Afraid that he will eventually be fired when he can no longer do his chores, he convinces George to let him join their dream of a farm because he can bring the necessary money to the scheme. He owns an old sheep dog that will become a symbol of Lennie before the novel ends.

Crooks The black stable worker who cares for the horses. A symbol of racial injustice, Crooks is isolated from the other hands because of his skin color. He also convinces Lennie to let him join their dream of land, but he must give up that dream.

Carlson The insensitive ranch hand who shoots Candy's dog. He owns a Luger, which George later uses to mercifully kill Lennie.

Curley The son of the ranch owner, Curley is a mean little guy who picks fights with bigger guys like Lennie. He is recently married and extremely jealous of any man who looks at or talks with his wife. Lennie crushes his hand, earning Curley's future enmity.

Curley's wife The only character in the novel who is given no name, she is Curley's possession. She taunts and provokes the ranch hands into talking with her, an action that causes Curley to beat them up. George sees her as a "tart," but Lennie is fascinated by her soft hair and looks. She is unsympathetically portrayed as a female tease until the final scene, in which the reader hears about her earlier dreams. Lonely and restless, she married too quickly to a husband who neglects her.

Character Map

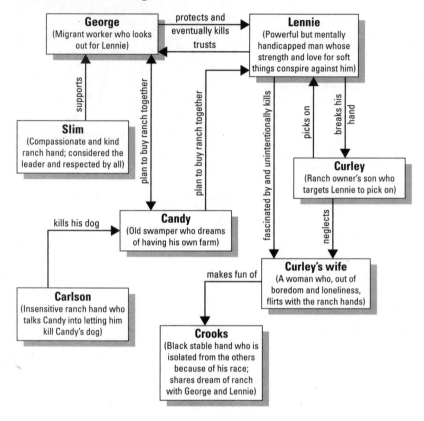

CRITICAL COMMENTARIES

Chapter One

Summary

Two men, dressed in denim jackets and trousers and wearing "black, shapeless hats," walk single-file down a path near the pool. Both men carry blanket rolls—called bindles—on their shoulders. The smaller, wiry man is George Milton. Behind him is Lennie Small, a huge man with large eyes and sloping shoulders, walking at a gait that makes him resemble a huge bear.

When Lennie drops near the pool's edge and begins to drink like a hungry animal, George cautions him that the water may not be good. This advice is necessary because Lennie is retarded and doesn't realize the possible dangers. The two are on their way to a ranch where they can get temporary work, and George warns Lennie not to say anything when they arrive. Because Lennie forgets things very quickly, George must make him repeat even the simplest instructions.

Lennie also likes to pet soft things. In his pocket, he has a dead mouse which George confiscates and throws into the weeds beyond the pond. Lennie retrieves the dead mouse, and George once again catches him and gives Lennie a lecture about the trouble he causes when he wants to pet soft things (they were run out of the last town because Lennie touched a girl's soft dress, and she screamed). Lennie offers to leave and go live in a cave, causing George to soften his complaint and tell Lennie perhaps they can get him a puppy that can withstand Lennie's petting.

As they get ready to eat and sleep for the night, Lennie asks George to repeat their dream of having their own ranch where Lennie will be able to tend rabbits. George does so and then warns Lennie that, if anything bad happens, Lennie is to come back to this spot and hide in the brush. Before George falls asleep, Lennie tells him they must have many rabbits of various colors.

Commentary

Steinbeck accomplishes a number of goals in the first chapter of his story. He sets the tone and atmosphere of the story's location, introduces his two main characters, begins some thematic considerations, adds imagery, and foreshadows later events in the story. All of this is accomplished with great economy and careful attention to word choices and repetition. When the story opens, for example, the setting is a few miles south of Soledad, California, near the Salinas River. "Soledad" is a Spanish word that translates into "loneliness" or "solitude," a reference to one of the novel's main themes.

Style & Language

Steinbeck's novel is written as though it is a play (in fact, after its publication, Steinbeck turned it into a play that opened on Broadway). The novel has six scenes (chapters), and each begins with a setting that is described in much the same way that a stage setting is described. For example, in the first "scene," there is a path, a sycamore tree near an ash pile from past travelers' fires, and a pool. All the action in this scene occurs in this one spot, much like a stage setting. After the main action in the scene, the focus pulls away from the action, preparing the reader for the next scene. In the first chapter, for example, when the characters settle down to sleep for the night, the focus pulls away from the men to the dimming coal of their campfire, to the hills, and finally to the sycamore leaves that "whispered in the little night breeze."

Steinbeck is a master of description, and one of his many passions was the California landscape. The setting in this novel contains the "golden foothill slopes" and the "strong and rocky Gabilan Mountains." It is quiet and natural with sycamores, sand, leaves, and a gentle breeze. The rabbits, lizards, and herons are out in this peaceful setting. The only signs of man are a worn footpath beaten hard by boys going swimming and tramps looking for a campsite, piles of ashes made by many fires, and a limb "worn smooth by men who have sat on it."

The two main characters are introduced first by their description and then with their names. Their physical portrayal emphasizes both their similarities and their individuality. They both wear similar clothes and carry blanket rolls, and the larger man imitates the smaller. But they are more dissimilar than they are alike: One is huge and shapeless; the other small and carefully defined. Lennie, the larger man, lumbers along heavily like a bear; George is small and has slender arms and small hands. The men also react differently to the pond: Lennie practically immerses himself in the water, snorting it up and drinking in long, greedy gulps. He fills his hat and puts it on his head, letting the water trickle merrily down his shoulders. George, on the other hand, is more cautious, wondering about the quality of the water before he drinks a small sample.

In their descriptions and interactions, Steinbeck shows the men's relationship: George takes care of Lennie, who is childlike and mentally handicapped, constantly giving him advice and instructions: Don't say anything tomorrow when we get to the ranch; come back here if there is any trouble; don't drink the water before you check out its quality; don't touch dead animals. But George also realizes that Lennie cannot remember or follow these simple instructions. George also carries Lennie's work card, knowing that Lennie would lose it. What George does not realize is how potentially dangerous Lennie is. All Lennie's transgressions thus far have been relatively minor: He has unintentionally killed a mouse and frightened the girl in Weed, but he has done so innocently. As will be discovered later, George mistakenly believes that he can protect Lennie from himself because Lennie will do anything George says. But Lennie's strength, his size, his mental handicap, and his fondness for soft things conspire against them.

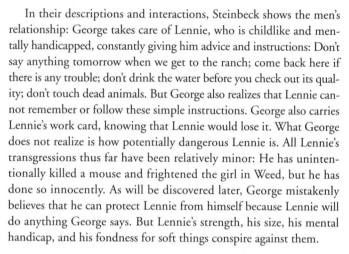

George seems to be of two minds when it comes to Lennie. He complains constantly that if he did not have Lennie he would be done with a huge responsibility. He could go to town, drink when he wanted, have a girlfriend, shoot pool, and, in general, have a life. Tired of constantly reminding Lennie of things he should remember, George gets quickly angry when Lennie forgets to get the firewood, for example, and instead goes after the dead mouse. On the other hand, George's anger is quickly under control, and he blames himself for scolding Lennie. In fact, Steinbeck makes clear that, despite his complaining and frustration, George looks out for Lennie and genuinely cares for him. The fact that George has repeated his instructions many times, the fact that he scolds Lennie for doing things (like petting the dead mouse or drinking the untested water) that could hurt him, and most importantly, the fact that George retells the story of their shared dream indicate the close relationship the two men have. In fact, George acts as a parent toward Lennie: He treats Lennie as one would treat a child, he laughs a great deal at Lennie's words, and because he knows how much Lennie likes soft things, he promises to try to get Lennie a puppy and to let him care for the rabbits when they finally get their own ranch.

A recurring motif in the novel is George and Lennie's dream of owning their own farm. It becomes obvious that these two men have traveled together for a long time because Lennie knows the words of the dream by heart, and he can finish the sentences even though he does not remember where he and George are going tomorrow. George's voice, echoing this dream, seems almost like a prayer. He emphasizes that the dream makes them special; they are different from other wandering migrants who have no family and no home. They have each other, and some day they will have a farm of their own where they can "live off the fatta the lan'." They are describing the American Dream of owning land, being independent, having material possessions that provide security, and, in general, running their own lives. Lennie's interpretation of this dream is that he will tend the rabbits—soft, furry animals that provide him with a feeling of security. This is a place where he won't be scared or running because he has "done a bad thing." Lennie's voice fills with laughter and happiness because safety means soft things and tending the rabbits.

Literary Device

Steinbeck also begins the animal imagery that will continue throughout his story. Lennie is often compared to a bear with his huge size and strength. His hands are described as paws, and he is always associated with rabbits and mice. He snorts like a horse at the stream and circles like a terrier when he does not want to bring the dead mouse to George. These animal images lead careful readers to question Lennie's future. With his enormous strength and his lack of intelligence, common sense, and responsibility, Lennie causes the reader to wonder how well he fits into human society. The title itself foreshadows the events that unfold and the ultimate tragedy of all the characters. Steinbeck thought about naming his story "Something That Happened." The stark, unfeeling title could easily fit the story's ending. Instead, he chose a phrase from Robert Burns' poem "To a Mouse On Turning Her Up in Her Nest with a Plow," November, 1785, which contains the following lines:

The best laid schemes o' mice and men

Gang aft a-gley [often go awry],

And lea'e us nought but grief and pain,

For promised joy.

Glossary

(Here, and in the following glossary sections, difficult words and phrases, as well as allusions and historical references, are explained.)

Soledad   a coastal California city about 130 miles south of San Francisco.

Salinas River a river that flows through Soledad and into Monterey Bay.

juncture a point or line of joining or connection.

mottled marked with blotches, streaks, and spots of different colors or shades.

recumbent biologically designating a part that leans or lies upon some other part or surface.

'coons short for "raccoons."

heron any of various wading birds with a long neck, long legs, and a long, tapered bill, living along marshes and river banks.

sweat-band a band, as of leather, inside a hat to protect the hat against damage from sweat.

bindle [Slang] a bundle, as of bedding, carried by a hobo.

morosely sullenly; gloomily.

work card a card with a job assignment usually given to workers by an employment agency. It is then presented to the employer by the worker.

Weed a northern California mining town.

bucking grain bags throwing heavy burlap bags of grain into a truck or wagon.

cat house [Slang] a house of prostitution.

jack [Old Slang] money.

Sacramento capital of California.

Chapter Two

Summary

The next morning, George and Lennie arrive at the ranch and go to the bunkhouse. The old swamper, Candy, informs them the boss is mad because they were supposed to arrive the night before. After Candy shows them which bunks to take, the conversation turns to people at the ranch, whom he describes.

When the boss arrives and questions Lennie and George about their work history and skills, George answers for Lennie, causing the boss to question Lennie's silence. George emphasizes Lennie's power and work ethic. Suspicious of their partnership, the boss asks George why they left their last job. George explains that the work was done. Satisfied, the boss leaves, telling them they can work after supper on Slim's grain team. After the boss leaves, George scolds Lennie for speaking.

The old swamper returns with an old sheep dog. George asks Candy about his dog. Candy says he raised the old dog from a pup and that he was a great sheep dog in his younger days.

Curley, the boss' son, enters and sizes up George. Looking at Lennie, Curley fists his hands and assumes a fighter's stance. He wants to know if they are the new guys, and when George answers, Curley insists that Lennie must talk when he is spoken to. Lennie repeats George's answer softly. Satisfied, Curley leaves to go look for his father.

With Curley gone, Candy explains that Curley used to be a lightweight fighter and now he hates big guys and picks fights with them. If that weren't bad enough, according to Candy, Curley has gotten much worse since his marriage two weeks earlier. Candy relates that Curley's wife is pretty but she has "got the eye," and she flirts with Slim and Carlson. Candy leaves, and George tells Lennie to stay away from Curley and not speak to him; however, George says, if Curley punches Lennie, Lennie is to "let him have it." Then George reminds Lennie of the place by the river where he is to go in case of trouble.

Shortly after, Curley's wife comes into the bunkhouse, claiming to look for Curley. Fascinated, Lennie can't take his eyes off her. Then Slim enters and tells her he saw Curley go into the house; Curley's wife becomes apprehensive and leaves.

When George says that Curley's wife seems like a "tramp," Lennie responds that he thinks she is "purty," causing George to warn Lennie to keep away from her, just like he's supposed to keep away from Curley. This admonition worries Lennie, who says, "I don't like this place, George. This ain't a good place." But George reminds him they must stay long enough to make a stake for their farm.

Another man, Carlson, enters the bunkhouse and asks Slim about his new puppies, suggesting that they could replace Candy's old dog, who is old, arthritic, and can barely walk or see, with one of the puppies. Hearing about the puppies, Lennie wants one too, and asks George to speak to Slim.

Supper is called. As Lennie gets off the bunk and approaches the door, Curley returns, looking for his wife. George tells him that she was there looking for Curley. George is afraid he will tangle with Curley himself as they all leave for supper.

Commentary

Theme

Chapter One began with a beautiful nature scene: the gentle breeze, the slopes of the mountains, the evening sun going down, and the calm pool. Chapter Two introduces the ranch. The bunkhouse is sparsely furnished; it's a dark room with just the essentials of a bunk and place to put gear. Once the story shifts from the natural setting of Chapter One to the bunkhouse in Chapter Two, things change considerably. Steinbeck contrasts the world of nature and the world of men. At the pond the water is warm, the breeze gentle, and the light shimmers over the sand. No wonder George wants to spend the night there instead of coming straight to the ranch. In contrast, the ranch contains characters who have been beaten down by life; it also contains danger in the form of Curley and his wife. By juxtaposing the natural scene at the pond with the scene in the bunkhouse, Steinbeck highlights the contrast between the freedom of nature and the unpredictable pattern of humans and their sometimes dangerous ways.

The atmosphere of the bunkhouse can be determined by the people George and Lennie meet there. Through the appearance of various characters, George and Lennie get a feeling for "the lay of the land." These characters represent various parts of American society during the Depression, and they also speak of some of the sadness of that time: loneliness, rootlessness, and poverty. Candy and Crooks, in particular, are characters separated from the others, Candy by old age and his hand-icap of only one hand, and Crooks because of his race. Yet when Candy reveals that the last guy (the one who had George's bunk) left because it was time to move on, we see the loneliness that plagues all the men who, like George and Lennie, move from place to place to find work. In this way, Steinbeck describes the general situation of the migrant hands; they work somewhere for a short time and move on to some other equally lonely place.

On three different occasions, characters express suspicion of Lennie and George traveling together. First, the boss questions whether or not George is using Lennie for his pay. The second person to question them is Curley, the boss' son. Rather than question their economic relation-ship, Curley hints that they have a sexual relationship. When he ques-tions George and George says "we travel together," Curley responds, "Oh, so it's that way." The third question comes from Slim, the "prince of the ranch," whose comment is in the form of a friendly statement rather than a question: "You guys travel around together?" When George answers that they look after each other, Slim says, "Ain't many guys travel around together . . . I don't know why. Maybe ever'body in the whole damn world is scared of each other."

Character Insight

This repetition of the same question serves two purposes: First, the fact that two men traveling together is unusual reinforces that the life of a migrant hand in the 1930s agricultural world is one of loneliness and rootlessness. Second, it provides insight into each of the charac-ters asking the question. The boss, by his presumption that George is taking Lennie's pay, shows him to be a man of business, interested solely in the bottom line. Curley, by his insinuation that the relation-ship is a sexual one, shows him to be base and cruel. Slim's reaction shows him to be the only one with the compassion to understand how traveling together might help the loneliness.

Literary Device

Throughout this chapter, Steinbeck pairs up various characters and situations. For example, the setting of the second chapter contrasts with the scene described at the beginning of Chapter One. Instead of calm and peace, Chapter Two has an air of menace largely caused by the presence of two characters on the ranch: Curley and his wife. While George can see the problems that may arise, Lennie can feel the men-acing atmosphere. After sizing up Lennie as a big guy but lacking in intelligence, Curley makes it a point to single out Lennie as someone who should speak when spoken to. Lennie immediately feels the men-ace, and the reader sees Curley right away as a bully.

The real problem, however, is Curley's wife. In addition to causing problems between the ranch hands and her husband, who has mandated that she not speak to anyone, she is fascinating to Lennie who sees only her prettiness and softness, not the danger she represents. George clearly sees the danger, however, and his immediate reaction to her is anger. He alternately calls her a "tramp," "bitch," "jailbait," "poison," and a "rattrap." His anger scares Lennie, who is fascinated with this creature he has never seen before.

The characters at this ranch also are paired, sometimes for the similarities they share (George and Candy, and Crooks and Candy); sometimes for the differences (Slim and Carlson). Slim, for example, is the sensitive, compassionate man whose word is law. Everyone respects him, and he seems to be the only one who is capable of understanding why George and Lennie travel together. Carlson, however, lovingly cleans his gun and is animalistic and insensitive. He is the one who thinks Candy's dog should be shot. Candy and Crooks represent another pair, because both are alienated from the others because of artificial barriers placed on them by society: one because he is old and crippled, the other because of the color of his skin. Both characters will later connect with George and Lennie's dream as a way out of their loneliness and alienation. Finally, George and Candy are paired. Both men are responsible and care for those unable to care for themselves: George is a caretaker for Lennie, and Candy is a caretaker of his old dog. While Carlson wants Slim to give Candy a pup to replace his old dog, George wants Slim to give Lennie a pup to take care of and pet. This final pairing is also important because it foreshadows the novel's final scene between George and Lennie.

Finally, in this chapter, Steinbeck has clearly delineated the lines of conflict—the menace coming from the evil and bullying of Curley and the seductive temptation of his wife. These two are catalysts of fear each time they appear. Even Lennie, who feels things instinctively, as an animal does, says, "I don't like this place, George. This ain't no good place. I wanna get outa here." In the second scene, the reader has only to wait for their eventual tragedy.

Glossary

whitewashed   painted with a mixture of lime, whiting, size, water, etc.

graybacks   [Slang] lice.

swamper here, a general handyman and person responsible for cleaning out the barn.

tick the cloth case or covering that is filled with cotton, feathers, hair, etc. to form a mattress or pillow.

sacking a cheap, coarse cloth woven of flax, hemp, or jute.

stable buck reference to Crooks, who is responsible for taking care of the horses.

skinner [Informal] a (mule) driver.

pugnacious eager and ready to fight; quarrelsome; combative.

in the ring in the sport or profession of boxing.

slough get rid of; in this case, to fire.

derogatory disparaging; belittling.

"she got the eye" said of Curley's wife, meaning that she flirts and is interested in men other than her husband.

tart a promiscuous woman.

stake a share or interest, as in property, a person, or a business venture.

mule a lounging slipper that does not cover the heel.

"he's eatin' raw eggs" refers to the notion that eating raw eggs increases sexual performance.

"writin' to the patent medicine houses" here, meaning that Curley is writing to mail-order businesses for medicines that increase sexual performance.

jerk-line skinner the main driver of a mule team, who handles the reins (jerk-line).

"on the wheeler's butt" on the rump of the wheel horse, the horse harnessed nearest the front wheels of a vehicle.

temple dancer a dancer known for delicate hand movements.

slang past tense of "sling," meaning to cast out; in this case, give birth to.

Chapter Three

Summary

Alone in the bunkhouse, George thanks Slim for giving Lennie a pup. Slim comments on Lennie's ability to work hard and mentions that it is obvious Lennie is not too bright. Slim then asks why Lennie and George go around together because most of the ranch hands he's seen are always alone and "[n]ever seem to give a damn about nobody."

Feeling comfortable with Slim, George explains that he knew Lennie's aunt. After her death, Lennie just naturally began staying with George and following him around. At first, George accepted Lennie's company because he could play jokes on Lennie, who didn't realize he was being made fun of. But one day, George told Lennie to jump into the Sacramento River, which Lennie did, even though he couldn't swim. Lennie nearly drowned before George was able to pull him out, and since then, no more jokes.

George also confides in Slim about Lennie's trouble in Weed: When Lennie touched a girl's dress, the girl screamed. Lennie got so scared that George had to hit him with a fence post to get him to let go. The girl claimed she had been raped, and so Lennie and George hid in an irrigation ditch and left in the night.

Carlson enters and complains bitterly about the smell of Candy's dog, offering to shoot it to put it out of its misery. Candy looks to the other guys, particularly Slim, for help with this decision. Slim sides with Carlson, and so Candy reluctantly lets Carlson take the dog out for execution.

Later, Crooks comes in, announcing that Lennie is petting the pups too much in the barn. Whit, another ranch hand, asks George if he has seen Curley's wife yet. George is noncommittal, and Whit remarks on her provocative dress. They discuss going into one of the town whorehouses that evening, and George tells Whit he might go but only to have a drink because he is saving his money for a stake.

Curley enters, looking for his wife. When he hears that she isn't there and that Slim is in the barn, he goes to the barn. Whit and Carlson follow, hoping for a fight. Disgustedly, George remarks that a whorehouse is a lot better for a guy than jailbait, and he mentions the story of a friend who ended up in prison over a "tart." Lennie loses interest and asks George once again about their farm.

Candy overhears their discussion and offers to contribute $300 toward the cost, if George and Lennie will let him join them. George eventually agrees, and then the three men muse on what their place will be like. They agree not to tell anyone of their plans. Candy admits he should have shot his dog himself.

The other guys filter back into the bunkhouse. Slim is angry at Curley for constantly asking about his wife. Curley, on the defensive and looking for someone to fight, picks a fight with Lennie and punches him unmercifully. Lennie doesn't protect himself until George tells him to fight back. When Lennie does, he crushes all the bones in Curley's hand.

Slim says they must get Curley to a doctor, but he cautions Curley that if he tells on Lennie and gets him fired, they will spread the word about how Curley's hand really got hurt and everyone will laugh at him. Badly shaken and in pain, Curley agrees not to tell. George explains to Slim that Lennie didn't mean to hurt Curley; he was just scared.

Because of what he has done, Lennie is afraid he won't get to tend the rabbits on their farm. George tells Lennie that it was not his fault and that he will get to tend the rabbits; then he sends Lennie off to wash his face.

Commentary

In Chapter Two, Lennie sensed that the ranch is not a safe place for them. Chapter Three brings that prophesy to light with a number of occurrences that are dark and violent. The death of Candy's dog and the crushing of Curley's hand are situations that have repercussions later. These dark images are balanced with Lennie's happiness in securing a puppy and the promise of being able to finally get their dream farm. Rather than alleviating the sense of foreboding, this juxtaposition of dark scenes with scenes full of promise serves to increase the reader's apprehension. The chapter ends with Curley's crushed hand and Lennie's (and George's) claims that Lennie didn't mean to hurt anyone, foreshadowing later events.

Character Insight

George and Lennie's relationship is further developed by Steinbeck in George's discussion with Slim. George makes his need for Lennie clear when he tells Slim about the incident at the river. George says, ". . . he'll do any damn thing I [tell him to do.]" Here the reader sees that George enjoys the opportunity to not only give Lennie advice, but also to be in charge. Lennie gives George stature. But now George uses that power carefully; he respects the fact that Lennie is not mean and would never intentionally hurt anyone. What George does not seem to realize is how dangerous Lennie's strength can be, a danger that Steinbeck makes clear when Lennie crushes Curley's hand.

Whit, a minor character, becomes important in this scene because he shows the life of a ranch hand when he isn't busy at his job. Whit reads pulp magazines, plays cards, and goes to Clara's or Susy's house on the weekend. He simply lives for today with no thought for his future and no concern for saving money, illustrating Steinbeck's point that sometimes our best intentions can be hurt by the human need for instant gratification or relief from the boredom.

Literary Device

Foreshadowing is heavy in this chapter with the repetition of the mens' attitudes toward Curley's wife. Whit asks George if he has seen her and ventures a comment on her appearance. Curley automatically assumes that she is in the barn with Slim, and the other guys follow him to the barn, assuming there will be a fight. George calls Curley's wife jailbait and refuses to go to the barn. He also mentions the story of Andy Cushman, a man who is now in prison because of a "tart." All of these events are Steinbeck's way of saying that something terrible is going to happen, and that Curley's wife will be involved.

In this chapter, the gloom is relieved by the hopeful planning of the three men—George, Lennie, and Candy—toward their dream. For the first time in his life, George believes the dream can come true with Candy's down payment. He knows of a farm they can buy, and the readers' hopes are lifted as well, as the men plan, in detail, how they will buy the ranch and what they will do once it is theirs. But while Steinbeck includes this story of hope, the preponderance of the chapter is dark. Both the shooting of Candy's dog and the smashing of Curley's hand foreshadow that the men will not be able to realize their dream.

Style & Language

The shooting of Candy's dog shows the callousness of Carlson and the reality of old age and infirmity. Carlson offers to shoot the old dog, complaining many times of the smell. He brutally keeps after Candy, and Candy's reaction can be seen in the adverbs Steinbeck uses to describe how Candy looks: "uneasily," "hopefully," "hopelessly." Candy reaches out to Slim for help, but even Slim says it would be better to put the dog down. "I wisht somebody'd shoot me if I get old an' a cripple" are the words Slim uses that Candy later echoes when he considers his own future.

Carlson is the stereotype of a macho male. He relentlessly pursues the dog's death, more for his own comfort (he doesn't like the dog's smell) than to put the dog out of its misery. He quickly and emphatically says he has a Luger that can do the job, and he has to be reminded by Slim to take a shovel so Candy will be spared the glimpse of the corpse. Carlson even cleans his gun in front of Candy after the deed is done. While it may be true that killing the dog put it out of its misery, little concern is shown for Candy's feelings after a lifetime of caring for the dog. Now Candy is like the rest of them—alone. The rough and brutal world of the ranch hand is revealed by Carlson's actions and then brought up once again with the brutality of Curley toward Lennie.

The unfortunate timing of Lennie's laughter is all the excuse Curley needs to fight the "big guy." Curley is a coward who would rather fight a big guy because, if he wins, he can brag about it, and if he is beaten, he doesn't lose face because the big guy should have picked on someone his own size. If Lennie were not mentally handicapped, he might have responded in a different way to the situation he finds himself in. But he is forced to make a scary choice, and, until George tells him to fight back, he simply takes the abuse. Lennie's fear is clearly on his face, and he says, "I didn't want to hurt him," when it is over. He does not really understand the repercussions of what has happened, and he is afraid that he has done "a bad thing." But the worst part of this whole scene is the uneasy feeling that somehow, somewhere, Curley will not forget this permanent injury, not only to his hand but also to his pride.

Glossary

derision   contempt or ridicule.

Auburn   a city about 35 miles northeast of Sacramento, California.

"rabbits in"   [Slang] jumps in.

pulp magazine   a magazine printed on rough, inferior paper stock made from wood pulp, usually containing sensational stories of love, crime.

euchre   a card game.

jailbait   [Slang] a young woman, considered a potential sexual partner, who has not reached the age of consent.

hoosegow [Slang] jail.

San Quentin a state prison, now closed, in the harbor of San Francisco.

raptly with a completely absorbed or engrossed look.

reprehensible deserving to be rebuked or scolded.

kick off die.

bemused plunged in thought; preoccupied.

"to bind her" to make a down payment.

welter short for "welterweight," a boxer between a junior welterweight and a junior middleweight.

Chapter Four

Summary

It is Saturday night, and Crooks is alone in his room when Lennie appears in the door. At first Crooks sends Lennie away, but eventually a conversation ensues in which Lennie says he came into the barn to see his pups, and Crooks warns Lennie that he is taking the pups from the nest too much. Lennie's disarming smile finally warms Crooks, and he lets Lennie stay and talk.

During their conversation, Lennie reveals the secret about the farm, which Crooks initially thinks Lennie is making up. Crooks also prods Lennie about his relationship with George and scares Lennie by suggesting that George might not come back. The more Crooks presses Lennie, the more Lennie becomes scared and upset. As Lennie circles dangerously close to Crooks, Crooks realizes the danger he is in and gently calms Lennie down, explaining that George is not hurt and that he was just "supposin'." Crooks then talks about his own loneliness.

Candy appears and talks with Lennie about the rabbits. Crooks interrupts and says they are kidding themselves about this farm because George is in town spending their money at a whorehouse. Exclaiming that the money is actually in the bank, Candy describes their farm where "couldn't nobody throw him off of it." Crooks asks to join their venture and says that he would work very hard and for no pay.

Curley's wife appears in the doorway, claiming that she is looking for Curley and complaining that she just wants someone to talk to. Candy says accusingly that she has a husband and she should not be fooling around with other men. When Curley's wife protests that Curley doesn't spend time with her, hates everyone else, and just talks about fighting, she suddenly remembers Curley's smashed hand and asks what happened to it. Candy tells her twice that Curley caught it in a machine, but she doesn't believe him.

Lennie watches her, fascinated, and Crooks keeps very quiet. Finally, Candy tells her to go away because she is not wanted in the barn. She will get them fired, he adds, and they don't need to hit the highway yet because they have other ideas, like getting their own place. At this revelation, Curley's wife laughs at the men and says it will never happen.

Before she leaves, she asks Lennie where he got the bruises on his face. Guiltily, Lennie says Curley got his hand caught in a machine. When she continues to talk to Lennie, Crooks tells her she has no right in his room and that he is going to tell the boss to keep her out. Curley's wife threatens Crooks with lynching. When Candy says that he and Lennie would tell on her for framing Crooks, she counters by saying no one will listen to the old swamper. The four then hear noise in the yard and realize the men are returning; Curley's wife tells Lennie she is glad he busted up Curley a bit, and then she leaves.

George appears, and Candy admits that he told Crooks about the farm. It is evident that George is not happy, and so the defeated Crooks tells Candy to forget his offer to help with the hoeing and doing odd jobs.

Commentary

This chapter begins with the description of a place; this time, it is Crooks' room in the stable. Crooks, the black stable hand, lives by himself in the harness room, a shed attached to the barn. Injured when a horse kicked him, Crooks has a body that is bent to the left because of his crooked spine. The stable hand has many horse care items in his room, as well as personal belongings he keeps because he is a more permanent tenant. Besides shoes, a clock, and a shotgun, Crooks also has a dictionary, a battered book of the California legal code, magazines, a few dirty books, and a pair of spectacles. Crooks' room is a source of pride, and he keeps it quite neat.

Character Insight

Crooks' room is a masterpiece of understatement, and its very nature shows how Crooks is different from the other ranch hands. Much of the room is filled with boxes, bottles, harnesses, leather tools, and other accouterments of his job. It is a room for one man alone. But scattered about on the floor are his personal possessions, accumulated because, unlike the other workers, he stays in this job. He has gold-rimmed spectacles to read (reading, after all, is a solitary experience). His pride and his self-respect are obvious from the neat, swept condition of his room. In his conversations are both the reality of accepting his solitary position and his anger at this condition. Candy, while around the place all the time, has never been in Crooks' room. The stable hand is not allowed in the bunkhouse because he is black. When he has an opportunity to wield some power of his own and hurt someone else as he has been hurt, Crooks takes the opportunity by picking on Lennie. But then sensing Lennie's fear and power, he backs down.

Through the description of Crook's room, his past life, and his current existence on the ranch, Chapter Four continues Steinbeck's themes of loneliness, barriers between people, and the powerlessness of the little guy in a huge world. Crooks describes his solitary life in terms of all the workers. He shares with Curley's wife the problem of no one with whom to talk. When Lennie questions him about the pups, Crooks changes the subject and mentions, "I seen it over an' over—a guy talkin' to another guy and it don't make no difference if he don't hear or understand. The thing is, they're talkin', or they're settin' still not talkin' . . . It's just bein' with another guy. That's all." Crooks can relate to the loneliness of the ranch hands. He goes back to his room and reads alone. "Sure you could play horseshoes till it got dark, but then you got to read books. Books ain't no good. A guy needs somebody—to be near him . . . . A guy goes nuts if he ain't got nobody. Don't make no difference who the guy is, long's he's with you . . . . I tell ya a guy gets too lonely an' he gets sick."

Crooks' loneliness is part of Steinbeck's microcosm of the world. Multiply Crooks a million times, and Steinbeck is pointing out the barriers and artificial obstacles people and society build against each other. Adding to Crooks' sense of powerlessness is his position, which is made clear by Curley's wife when she breaks up their little gathering. When Crooks tries to get her to leave because her presence is sure to cause trouble, she tells him, "Well, you keep your place then, Nigger. I could get you strung up on a tree so easy it ain't even funny." Crooks knows that she is absolutely correct; in fact, once she uses her position as Curley's white wife as a weapon, Crooks dissolves into nothingness. Steinbeck describes him growing smaller, pressing himself against the wall, and trying to avoid the hurt. As Steinbeck states, "Crooks had retired into the terrible protective dignity of the Negro." Candy with his old age, Lennie with his retardation, Crooks with his race, Curley's wife with her gender: all are victims of the attitudes and prejudices of society.

Crooks is not only a realist about his position in society, but he is also prophetic about George and Lennie's dream. Like the many other migrants he has seen come and go, Crooks tells Candy that he has never seen one realize their dream for land. The reason they do not get the land is stated clearly by Crooks and echoed by Curley's wife. Crooks explains, "I seen guys nearly crazy with loneliness for land, but ever' time a whorehouse or a blackjack game took what it takes." This pronouncement is played out in Whit's and the rest of the hands' behavior on Saturday night: All have gone into town. They never see beyond the end of the week. Curley's wife reinforces this idea when she tells them "If you had two bits in the worl', why you'd be in gettin' two shots of corn with it and suckin' the bottom of the glass. I know you guys."

Literary Device

It is always the dream of the powerless to have a little land where they can make their own decisions and be their own bosses. In this case, having their own place would ease the loneliness and put a damper on Candy's fear that he'll be turned out when he's too old to work, Crooks' fear he'll be gone because of his race and bad back, and George and Lennie's desire to be free of the boss and do what their hearts desire. But Crooks certainly tells the reality of the story in one of the most poignant speeches in the novel: "Just like heaven. Ever'-body wants a little piece of lan'. I read plenty of books out here. Nobody never gets to heaven, and nobody gets no land. It's just in their head. They're all the time talkin' about it, but it's jus' in their head." This speech foreshadows George's plight at the end of the book.

Glossary

California civil code   a book of civil law for the state of California.

aloof   distant in sympathy, interest, etc.; reserved and cool.

meager   of poor quality or small amount; not full or rich.

took a powder   [Slang] ran away; left.

booby hatch   [Slang] an institution for the mentally ill.

nail keg   a barrel for holding nails.

"roll your hoop"   a reference to a child's game. Candy is saying Curley's wife is just a child.

Chapter Five

Summary

Lennie is alone inside the barn, stroking a dead puppy. Worried that George will find out and won't let him tend the rabbits, Lennie buries the dead pup in the hay and says that he will claim to have found it dead. But then he uncovers the pup and strokes it again, realizing that George will know he killed it because George always knows and Lennie won't get to tend the rabbits. Lennie becomes so angry that he hurls the dead puppy across the barn. Shortly after having thrown the puppy, Lennie picks it up again, stroking it and deciding that maybe George won't care.

Curley's wife enters the barn and asks Lennie what he has. Lennie repeats George's instructions that he is not to talk to her. She stays, however, and again asks him what he is covering up. When Lennie shows her the dead puppy, she tells him it was just a mutt and no one will care, but Lennie explains that George won't let him tend the rabbits because he did a bad thing again.

Curley's wife tells Lennie of her life and her missed opportunity to travel with the show that came through her hometown. Lennie responds absently with concern about his dream farm and the rabbits he will have. Following his comment, Curley's wife chatters on, explaining more about her lost chance to become an actress and how she met Curley. As she talks, she moves closer, confiding in him about the life she might have had. Lennie, however, is still trying to figure out how to get rid of the dead pup so that George won't know.

When Lennie explains that he likes to pet soft things, Curley's wife reveals that she too likes to feel silk and velvet, and she invites him to feel her hair, which is very soft. He does, but his big, clumsy fingers start to mess it up, and she angrily tells him to let go. As she tries to get her hair away from Lennie, he becomes scared and holds on more tightly. When she begins to scream, Lennie covers her mouth with his hand. A struggle ensues—Lennie panicking and Curley's wife's eyes "wild with terror"—until her body flops "like a fish" and then she is still.

When Lennie realizes that she is dead, he panics and paws the hay to partially cover her. Hearing the horseshoe game outside, he understands that someone will come in sooner or later and discover the bad thing he has done. Immediately he remembers to hide in the brush until George comes. Picking up the dead pup, he leaves to go to the hiding place.

Candy finds Curley's wife and runs out to find George, who, upon seeing the body, knows what happened. George considers what will happen to Lennie: They could lock Lennie up, but he'd starve, and people would be mean to him. Candy says they need to let Lennie get away because Curley will lynch him, but George realizes how hopeless escape would be. He tells Candy to give him a minute to go to the bunkhouse before telling the other men; then George will come along as though he had not already seen Curley's wife.

Candy asserts that he and George can still have their farm, but George realizes that it will never happen. Now George has no dream, and he will end up working like the other ranch hands and spending his money in a poolroom or "some lousy cat house."

Carlson, Whit, Curley, and Crooks come back in the barn with Candy and, following them, George. Curley immediately blames Lennie, saying he will go for his shotgun and shoot Lennie in the guts. Carlson follows Curley out of the barn, going for his Luger. When Slim asks George where Lennie might be, George tells Slim Lennie would have gone south (knowing all along that the little pool is north of the ranch). When George claims that they might find Lennie first and bring him in and lock him up, Slim explains that Curley will want to kill him, and even if he doesn't, how would Lennie like being locked up and strapped down like an animal in a cage?

Carlson and Curley return, and Carlson claims that Lennie has stolen his Luger. Curley, carrying a shotgun, tells Carlson to take Crooks' shotgun, and the men leave, taking George with them to find Lennie.

Commentary

Chapter Five is filled with characters whose thoughts can be described very precisely: Lennie's fear, Curley wife's musings and then her terror, George's stoic acceptance, Curley's meanness, and Candy's despondency. All occur because of the meeting in the barn between Lennie and Curley's wife, a meeting that seals forever the fates of all involved.

Character Insight

Lennie's fate is sealed when he realizes he has done a worse thing than kill a pup. His panic in killing Curley's wife is much like the panic he felt when Curley baited him and Lennie broke Curley's hand. Lennie differentiates at some level between the bad thing of killing the pup and the bad thing of killing Curley's wife, as evidenced by his leaving for the bushes near the river when he realizes she is dead. However, he doesn't fully comprehend the implications of her death, as evidenced by his taking the pup's body with him so that George wouldn't see it as well. Lennie's reasoning is that the body of Curley's wife is bad enough; the body of the pup would compound the wrong done. This action—and the thought process that preceded it—reemphasizes Lennie's childlike understanding of the events that have transpired.

Character Insight

Throughout the novel, Steinbeck describes Curley's wife in terms of her appearance and the reactions of the ranch hands toward her. She has been alternately a "tart," "jailbait," and various other derogatory terms, used often by George. But in this scene, the reader gets a different view of her as she talks about her own lost dreams. Her current situation is the result of a series of bad choices and unhappy circumstance. She lost her chance at being in the movies because of her age and her mother, and, perhaps in retaliation, she took up with Curley, leading to a loveless marriage with a man who abuses her and completes her feelings of worthlessness. She lives a solitary life on a ranch, with no companion, no one to talk to, and in continual fear that her husband will beat up any person in sight. Although her actions and flirtations have exacerbated the unhappiness of her situation, Steinbeck gives us a view of her past, and we discover that she, like everyone else in the novel—and perhaps even more so—is a victim of loneliness.

Style & Language

Steinbeck reinforces this kinder impression of Curley's wife in his description of her in death. Momentarily, the light from the setting sun becomes softer and shines across her body. She no longer looks like a tart who needs attention; instead she looks like a young, pretty, innocent girl, sleeping lightly.

George clearly accepts the end of his and Lennie's dream. The reader feels that he never really believed it could happen even though the plan of using Candy's money made it seem possible for awhile. George says on two different occasions to Candy, "I should of knew . . . I guess maybe way back in my head I did." Later when Candy suggests they could still have the farm together, George says, ". . . I think I knowed from the very first. I think I know'd we'd never do her. He usta like to hear about it so much I got to thinking maybe we would." Without Lennie, the dream is gone and perhaps never really existed except in the words that made Lennie's happiness complete.

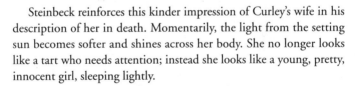

George's words echo the prophesy of Crooks when he imagines what his life will be like without Lennie: "I'll work my month an' I'll take my fifty bucks an' I'll stay all night in some lousy cat house. Or I'll set in some poolroom till ever'body goes home. An' then I'll come back an' work another month an' I'll have fifty bucks more." Gone is the dream. Gone are the complaints about what he could do if he did not have Lennie around his neck. Now he will be alone like everyone else.

Glossary

four-taloned Jackson fork   a hay fork with four prongs, for lifting large amounts of hay.

Salinas   city in west central California, near Monterey.

"in the pitcher"   "in the picture;" here, meaning in the movies.

ringer   a horseshoe thrown so that it encircles the peg.

Chapter Six

Summary

Lennie is by the deep pool of the Salinas River, waiting for George. He talks to himself, repeating that George will be mad and give him hell. From his memory, he creates his Aunt Clara, who stares disapprovingly and scolds him because once again he did not listen to George. Then Aunt Clara disappears and is replaced in Lennie's mind by a giant rabbit, who takes Aunt Clara's job of scolding Lennie and tells him he cannot tend the rabbits and that George will beat Lennie with a stick. Lennie protests that George has never "raised his han' to me with a stick." But the rabbit persists, and Lennie puts his hands over his ears and calls out for George.

Coming silently through the bushes, George asks Lennie what he is yelling about. Lennie describes his fears of George leaving and confesses that he has once again done a bad thing. Strangely silent, George explains that it does not matter this time. Then Lennie asks for "the story" about how they are different from the other guys. George takes his hat off and asks Lennie to do so too; then he tells Lennie to look across the river while he tells him their dream once again.

While Lennie listens happily to the story, George pulls Carlson's Luger and unsnaps the safety. George explains to Lennie that everyone will be nice to him on their place and there won't be any trouble or theft. When Lennie says he thought George would be mad, George tells him he never was and the important thing he wants Lennie to know is that he is not mad now. Then George brings up the gun to Lennie's neck and pulls the trigger. Lennie falls forward on the sand, and George throws the gun away from him into an old pile of ashes.

The men hear the shot and run up, Slim's voice calling to George. They burst into the clearing, Curley in the lead. The men assume Lennie had Carlson's gun and George numbly agrees. Slim touches George's elbow and says they should go for a drink. Then, as he helps George up, he says to him that he had to do what he did. Slim leads George up to the trail and on toward the highway, leaving Carlson to wonder—along with Curley—Now what the hell ya suppose is eatin' them two guys?"

Commentary

In Chapter Six, the story ends where it began, but the values of the setting have changed. Instead of a place of sanctuary, the pool is now a place of death. Instead of the rabbits playing in the brush, the heron is swallowing the little snake whole. Instead of green leaves and a gentle breeze, there are brown, dying leaves and a gush of wind. Instead of safety for Lennie, there is death. Instead of companionship for George, there is a future of loneliness.

Character Insight

Lennie experiences two visions in this last scene. One is Aunt Clara who scolds Lennie for letting George down and not listening to him. The other is a gigantic rabbit who berates Lennie and tells him George will beat him and leave him. In neither of these visions does Lennie experience feelings of remorse or guilt for what he did to Curley's wife. In fact, neither his conjured Aunt Clara or the giant rabbit scold him for that act. In regards to Curley's wife, Lennie simply knows that he "did a bad thing" and that the consequences will be severe. His thoughts, though, focus on the pattern he and George have established when Lennie does bad things: George scolds him, threatens to leave him, and then ends up telling him once again about their dream of a ranch. The fact that Lennie anticipates the same pattern this time is indicative of his childlike innocence. Instead of asking George right away for the story of the farm, he asks him for the story of "giving me hell." He knows this will make George feel better, and everything will be alright again.

George, however, cannot finish the story of what he would do without Lennie. He falters, realizing that soon he truly will be without Lennie. When Lennie realizes that George is not going to beat him or leave him, he playfully finishes the story, and he adds why they are different from the others: "An' I got you. We got each other, that's what, that gives a hoot in hell about us." Now the story of the ranch and the dream is the only one left, and George begins that, picturing a world where no one will steal from them or be mean. But, of course, this story is not reality in a cold, harsh world. There is no place for innocence or people who look out for each other. As Lennie envisions the dream that seemed so close a few days ago, George shoots him as Carlson shot Candy's dog, and like the dog, without a quiver, Lennie dies.

Literary Device

Earlier in the novel, Slim told Candy it would be better to put his dog down, better for their "society" as a whole. This comment begins a number of comparisons between Candy's dog and Lennie. George never really understood how dangerous Lennie could be and always thought Lennie's strength could be restrained. Now it is obvious that Lennie is a danger to society, even though innocent in the motivations for his actions. Candy had no other merciful options for his dog, and George sees no other options for Lennie. As Slim explained, locking Lennie up would be inhumane; Curley threatens to harm Lennie by shooting him many times. When Carlson shot Candy's dog, he displayed no concern for Candy's feelings. The same is true for the others' reactions to Lennie's death. Carlson and the others cannot fathom why George is upset. The final similarity in the two situations is the fearful future of loneliness facing both Candy and George.

When the ranch hands appear, George lies about the murder. He quietly concurs that Lennie had Carlson's gun. George feels numb and empty, but he has done what he felt he had to do. Slim understands, taking him for a drink. But Carlson and Curley can not understand why George feels so bad. Their last words—"Now what the hell ya suppose is eatin' them two guys?"—indicate that the world is a cold and harsh place.

Glossary

jack-pin   a metal or wooden pin used to fasten ropes to a ship.

CHARACTER ANALYSES

George Milton

George is described as physically small with very sharp features, an opposite to Lennie Small. Milton is the last name of the author of one of Steinbeck's favorite works, *Paradise Lost*. In that epic poem, Adam and Eve fall from grace in the Garden of Eden. Because of their fall, mankind is doomed to be alone and walk the earth as a lonely being. Some critics believe George represents that doomed man who longs to return to Eden. His one chance to avoid that fate is his relationship with Lennie, which makes them different from the other lonely men. But despite this companionship, at the end of the book, George is fated to be once again alone.

George's personality often reflects both anger and understanding. Of the two men, he is the one who thinks things through and considers how their goals can be reached. Once Candy makes the stake possible, George comes up with the details: where they will get the ranch, how long they must work to pay for it, and how they will have to keep a low profile in order to work for the next month. George also foresees possible complications and gives Lennie advice about what he must do in order to help their future. While George can be very rational and thoughtful, he also gets frustrated and angry with Lennie because the big man cannot control his strength or actions. George repeatedly gets angry, so much so that Lennie knows by heart what it means when George "gives him hell." But George's anger quickly fades when he remembers Lennie's innocence and his inability to remember or think clearly.

George, unlike other men, has a companion and friend in Lennie. Because of this, Lennie makes George feel special. They are different from all the other guys, and George realizes only too well that they have a special bond. At the ranch, George often plays solitaire, a game for one. Without Lennie, George would be a loner. Even though George gets frustrated by Lennie's mental weakness, he also feels compassion for his friend. Lennie offers George the opportunity to lay plans, give advice, and, in general, be in charge. Without Lennie, George would be just like the other hands, but with Lennie, George has a strong sense of responsibility. In the end, he even takes responsibility for Lennie's death. George also understands that Lennie does not have an adult's sense of guilt and does not understand death or murder beyond it being a "bad thing." George makes it possible for Lennie—sometimes—to understand at least partial consequences of his actions. Unfortunately, George does not realize how dangerous Lennie can be, and this lack of foresight adds to the downfall of their dream.

Their dream also sets George apart from the others because it means he and Lennie have a future and something to anticipate. Unlike Lennie, George does not see their dream in terms of rabbits; instead, he sees it in a practical way. Their farm will be one where they can be independent and safe and where he will not have to worry about keeping track of Lennie's mistakes. They can be secure and in charge of their own lives. However, Lennie is the one who adds the enthusiasm because George never really believed they could swing this farm of their own. He mostly uses the story to give Lennie something to believe in for their future. Only when Candy offers the stake does George actually begin to see that this dream could come true. But, realist that he is, George tells Candy over the lifeless body of Curley's wife, "I think I knowed from the very first. I think I know'd we'd never do her. He usta like to hear about it so much I got to thinking maybe we would [be able to have the farm.]" In the end, George Milton is man alone once again.

Lennie Small

Lennie Small is huge and lumbering and, in many ways, the opposite of George Milton. Where George has sharp features and definite lines, Lennie is "shapeless." Often he is described in terms of animals. He lumbers like a bear and has the strength of a bear, but his actions are often described like those of a dog.

Lennie's personality is like that of a child. He is innocent and mentally handicapped with no ability to understand abstract concepts like death. While he acts with great loyalty to George, he has no comprehension of the idea of "loyalty." For that reason, he often does not mean to do the things that get him into trouble, and once he does get into trouble, he has no conscience to define his actions in terms of guilt. Lennie only defines them in terms of consequences: "George is going to give me hell" or "George won't let me tend the rabbits." He is devoted to George like a dog is devoted to its master, and he tries to follow George's commands. There is a childlike wonder in Lennie that can be seen when he first sees the pool of water and slurps down huge gulps of water like a horse.

Lennie's greatest feeling of security comes from petting soft things. When the rest of the world gets complicated and scary, petting soft things helps Lennie feel safe. In petting dead mice, Lennie is doing something that makes him feel safe. Society as a whole would disapprove of what he is doing, but Lennie sees nothing wrong in his actions.

When they have their farm, as George tells him at the end, Lennie will not need to be scared of bad things any more, and he can tend the rabbits and pet them.

Lennie's prodigious strength combined with his lack of intelligence and conscience make him dangerous, and he needs George to keep him out of trouble. George takes care of Lennie and makes the decisions for him. George also gives him advice and helps Lennie when overwhelming forces, like Curley, scare him. George keeps the dream out in front of the huge man as a goal: Their farm is a place where they can live together, have animals, grow their own crops and, in general, feel safe. Lennie has little memory, but the story of their dream is one he knows by heart. While George never really believes in this farm, Lennie embraces it with childlike enthusiasm. Every time he makes George tell their story, his enthusiasm excites George, too. Lennie's innocence keeps the dream alive, but his human imperfection makes the dream impossible to realize.

Candy

Candy is "a tall, stoop-shouldered old man . . . . He was dressed in blue jeans and carried a big push-broom in his left hand." His right hand is simply a stump because he lost his hand in a ranch accident. Now the owners of the ranch keep him on as long as he can "swamp" out or clean the bunkhouse. Candy gives Steinbeck an opportunity to discuss social discrimination based on age and handicaps. Candy represents what happens to everyone who gets old in American society: They are let go, canned, thrown out, used up. Candy's greatest fear is that once he is no longer able to help with the cleaning he will be "disposed of." Like his old dog, he has lived beyond his usefulness.

Candy and his dog parallel the relationship of George and Lennie. Like Candy's dog, Lennie depends on George to take care of him and show him what to do. Candy, like George, is different from the other ranch hands because he has his dog as a constant companion, someone devoted and loyal to him. When the unfeeling Carlson suggests that Candy's dog be put out of its misery, Candy abdicates the responsibility to Carlson. He tells George later that he should have shot his dog himself, foreshadowing George's decision to take responsibility for Lennie's death and "be his brother's keeper."

Candy also plays a significant role in the dream, providing the money needed to make the down payment. Because of Candy, the dream almost becomes real. Candy's down payment causes George to believe that, perhaps, the dream can be realized. But none of them count on the tragic meeting between Curley's wife and Lennie in the barn. Even then Candy still thinks he can have his safe haven, a place where no one will throw him out when he is too old. The dream is so strong in him that he pleads with George, to no avail, to have their farm despite Lennie's death.

Curley

Curley, the boss' son, is an evil character in Steinbeck's world. Even Lennie feels the sense of menace when Curley first comes into the bunkhouse. Curley is a "thin young man with a brown face, with brown eyes and a head of tightly curled hair." According to Candy, Curley is an amateur boxer and is always picking fights, especially with guys who are bigger than he is.

Curley tries to prove his masculinity by picking fights. Another way to prove himself is by marrying a physically attractive woman. His wife is never given a name, but by calling her "Curley's wife," Steinbeck indicates she is his possession. Curley refuses to let her talk to anyone on the ranch, isolating her from everyone and setting the stage for trouble. He makes a big show of keeping his hand soft to caress her, yet patronizes the local whorehouse on Saturday night. While he may strut around the ranch because of his position as the boss' son, he obviously cannot satisfy his wife and is mean to her. Curley beats up any man who dares to talk to her; the only one he listens to and seems to respect is Slim.

When Curley picks the fight with Lennie, he does not realize the danger he is in. Once George allows Lennie to fight back, Lennie smashes Curley's hand, breaking every bone. Curley whimpers like a baby and cries helplessly with the pain. When Lennie kills Curley's wife, Curley sees this as his opportunity for revenge. In his meanness, he tells Carlson to aim for Lennie's gut so that Lennie will suffer. This, in turn, causes George to make the decision to kill Lennie mercifully.

Curley's Wife

Curley's wife, like the other players in the drama, is simply a character type and the only woman in the plot. She is defined by her role: Curley's wife or possession. George and Candy call her by other names such as "jailbait" or "tart." She wears too much makeup and dresses like a "whore" with red fingernails and red shoes with ostrich feathers. Lennie is fascinated by her and cannot take his eyes off her. He keeps repeating "she's purty." George, realizing Lennie's fascination, warns him to stay away from her.

Curley's wife knows her beauty is her power, and she uses it to flirt with the ranch hands and make her husband jealous. She is utterly alone on the ranch, and her husband has seen to it that no one will talk to her without fearing a beating.

Steinbeck's initial portrayal of Curley's wife shows her to be a mean and seductive temptress. Alive, she is connected to Eve in the Garden of Eden. She brings evil into mens' lives by tempting them in a way they cannot resist. Eventually, she brings about the end of the dream of Eden, the little farm where George and Lennie can live off the fat of the land. Her death at Lennie's hands means the end of George and Lennie's companionship and their dream. She is portrayed, like the girl in Weed, as a liar and manipulator of men. In the scene in Crooks' room, she reminds Crooks of his place and threatens to have him lynched if he doesn't show her the proper respect as the wife of the boss' son and a white woman. All of these appearances cause the reader to dislike her and see her as the downfall of the men in the story.

In the barn scene, however, Steinbeck softens the reader's reaction to Curley's wife by exploring her dreams. Her "best laid plans" involved a stint in the movies with all the benefits, money, and pleasure that would provide. Her beauty is such that perhaps that dream might have come true. Her dreams make her more human and vulnerable. Steinbeck reiterates this impression by portraying her innocence in death:

> Curley's wife lay with a half-covering of yellow hay. And the meanness and the plannings and the discontent and the ache for attention were all gone from her face. She was very pretty and simple, and her face was sweet and young. Now her rouged cheeks and her reddened lips made her seem alive and sleeping very lightly. The curls, tiny little sausages, were spread on the hay behind her head, and her lips were parted.

Steinbeck seems to show, through Curley's wife, that even the worst of us have our humanity.

Slim

Slim is described always in terms of dignity and majesty. When he first comes into the bunkhouse, he moves "with a majesty achieved only by royalty and master craftsmen. He was a jerk-line skinner, the prince of the ranch, capable of driving ten, sixteen, even twenty mules with a single line to the leaders." Slim is tall, ageless, and an expert in his job. His voice is the voice of rationalism. When Carlson suggests killing Candy's dog, Candy appeals to Slim as the final authority.

Slim is so respected and admired on the ranch that even Curley listens to him. When Lennie smashes Curley's hand, Slim is the one who intercedes and tells Curley he will not have George and Lennie fired. Slim understands Curley's fear of ridicule, and he uses that fear to help George and Lennie. Slim also inspires confidences because he is not judgmental. When George first meets Slim, George tells him about Lennie's troubles in Weed. George senses in Slim a person of intelligence and empathy who will not be mean to Lennie, make fun of him, or take advantage of him.

Slim is the only one on the ranch who appreciates the difficulty of George's position. He understands the constant oversight George must exercise in watching Lennie and keeping him out of trouble. It is Slim, in the end, who suggests that George did the right thing in killing Lennie mercifully. He explains the alternative: "An s'pose they lock him up an' strap him down and put him in a cage. That ain't no good, George."

Slim is present at every crucial juncture in the story: the death of Candy's dog, the smashing of Curley's hand, finding the body of Curley's wife, at the pool after George has shot Lennie. In each case, there is violence or the threat of it. Each time Slim helps make the assessment to do what is merciful or what is right.

Crooks

Crooks is so named because of a crooked back caused by a kick from a horse. Crooks is the stable hand who takes care of the horses and lives by himself because he is the only black man on the ranch. Along with Candy, Crooks is a character used by Steinbeck to show the effects of discrimination. This time the discrimination is based on race, and Crooks is not allowed in the bunkhouse with the white ranch hands. He has his own place in the barn with the ranch animals. Candy realizes he has never been in Crooks' room, and George's reaction to Crooks being involved in their dream is enough to cause Crooks to withdraw his request to be part of the dream. Racial discrimination is part of the microcosm Steinbeck describes in his story. It reaches its height in the novel when Curley's wife puts Crooks "in his place" by telling him that a word from her will have him lynched. Interestingly, only Lennie, the flawed human, does not see the color of Crooks' skin.

Crooks also has pride. He is not the descendent of slaves, he tells Lennie, but of landowners. In several places in the story, Steinbeck shows Crook's dignity and pride when he draws himself up and will not "accept charity" from anyone. Crooks also displays this "terrible dignity" when Curley's wife begins to tear away at his hope for the dream farm.

Crooks is not without his faults, however. He scares Lennie and makes up the story of George leaving him. Prejudice isn't simply a characteristic of the white ranch hands or the daughter-in-law of the boss; it is a human characteristic, and Crooks needs to feel superior to someone also.

That he becomes part of the dream farm is an indication of Crooks' loneliness and insecurity. He, like Candy, realizes that once he is no longer useful he will be "thrown out." Where, then, can he find some security for his future? The dream farm of Lennie's seems to be the place. Crooks promises to work for nothing as long as he can live his life out there without the fear of being put out. Like all the others, he wants a place where he can be independent and have some security. But there is no security for anyone in a prejudiced world, least of all a black stable hand with a crooked back.

CRITICAL
ESSAYS

Structure of the Novel

Steinbeck wrote *Of Mice and Men* in a play format, using a circular pattern of locales, condensed narration, minimal action descriptions, dramatic lighting, and foreshadowing to connect his plot. Some readers feel that *Of Mice and Men* is so balanced and thoughtful in structure that the novel is a work of art. Other readers feel that the structure makes the book predictable, taking away from the reader's interest.

Nevertheless, Steinbeck's novel easily translated to the stage, almost intact, because of his thoughtful craftsmanship. The locales are perfectly balanced in a circular pattern. There are six scenes in groups of two, producing three "acts." The first and last scene take place near the bank of the river so that the plot comes full circle. In the middle are two scenes in the bunkhouse, and two scenes in the barn, the latter including Crooks' room which is in the barn.

In each of these scenes, Steinbeck develops an interesting pattern of general to specific. For example, in the first scene by the river, Steinbeck begins with a "camera shot" of the entire scene so the reader can take in the mountains, the sun, the river, and all of nature in the vicinity. Then he focuses in on a path and then—still more—on two men walking down that path. At the end of the first scene the author does just the opposite. The focus is on the two men settling down for the night and then the "camera" pulls out and expands the scene to include the night, the fire, and hills. A close examination of each scene will bring the reader to the conclusion that Steinbeck has produced a well balanced pattern that beautifully supports his plot and themes.

Two other stage conventions include the entrances and exits by characters and, at the beginning of each scene, the setting descriptions. In each scene are entrances and exits by the characters. For example, when Chapter Four opens, Crooks is sitting in his room applying liniment to his back. Next, Lennie appears in the open doorway, waiting to be asked in. Eventually, other characters make entrances: Candy and Curley's wife. Then Curley's wife exits, George enters, and the three men exit, leaving Crooks alone once again.

A dramatic format is used also for the beginning of scenes. Each starts with a sparse description of the setting, much like a playwright would do at the beginning of a play scene. The first and last scenes have descriptions of nature and set the atmosphere for the action. In between these scenes are brief setting descriptions of the bunkhouse and Crooks' room in the barn and the barn itself.

The whole novel contains very little narration. Instead, Steinbeck relies heavily on the words and actions of his characters. A careful study of each chapter reveals that, after the initial description of the setting, most pages contain almost all dialogue with very short introductory phrases. Steinbeck wants readers to draw their own conclusions about the characters and the themes from the action and words of the people, rather than from Steinbeck's opinions. Thus Steinbeck uses a technique that helps his novel translate easily to a staged production.

Within each scene is a pattern of rising and falling action. In the second scene, for example, the bunkhouse and inhabitants are introduced, suspicion falls on the two men's relationship, Curley and his wife inject an ominous tone (which Lennie repeats with his instinctive reaction to them), Slim soothes the scene, and then they go to dinner. Again, each scene is balanced with this theatrical structure.

The lighting could also be attributed to theatrical technique. The first and last scenes use the light in nature for the focus of the lighting in the scenes. In the third chapter, the bunkhouse is dark, and it is evening. When George and Slim come in, Slim turns on the electric light over the card table. The focus is on the conversation at the card table with the darkness all around. From that darkness, come the voices of Lennie and Candy, but the main focus of the scene is in the middle of the room at the card table where the light is used to draw the reader's attention to the main arena of action. Light and darkness work through the novel to focus the reader's attention, much like light and darkness on the stage accomplish a similar purpose.

A final structural technique is the use of foreshadowing, or transitional connections or signals, to connect and make ideas more fluid. Throughout Steinbeck's novel, there is so much foreshadowing that some critics feel he has over used the technique. As an example, Candy's dog and the circumstances surrounding its death are later repeated in the death of Lennie. The same technique is used when George warns Lennie very early to go back to the bushes by the pool if anything bad happens. This advice is repeated several times in other scenes, including Lennie's thoughts in the barn and later at the pool while waiting for George.

Overall, Steinbeck's novel is tightly structured and intentionally written in an arrangement that uses theatre conventions to produce unity and convey a message.

The Themes of the Novel

Much like Steinbeck's short novel *The Pearl, Of Mice and Men* is a parable that tries to explain what it means to be human. His friend Ed Ricketts shaped Steinbeck's thinking about man's place in the universe. Essentially, man is a very small part of a very large universe; in the greater scheme of things, individuals come and go and leave very little, lasting mark. Yet deep inside all people is a longing for a place in nature—the desire for the land, roots, and a place to call "home." The struggle for such a place is universal, and its success is uncertain.

In sharing his vision of what it means to be human, Steinbeck touches on several themes: the nature of dreams, the nature of loneliness, man's propensity for cruelty, powerlessness and economic injustices, and the uncertainty of the future.

The Nature of Dreams

In essence, *Of Mice and Men* is as much a story about the nature of human dreams and aspirations and the forces that work against them as it is the story of two men. Humans give meaning to their lives—and to their futures—by creating dreams. Without dreams and goals, life is an endless stream of days that have little connection or meaning. George and Lennie's dream—to own a little farm of their own—is so central to *Of Mice and Men* that it appears in some form in five of the six chapters. In fact, the telling of the story, which George has done so often, becomes a ritual between the two men: George provides the narrative, and Lennie, who has difficulty remembering even simple instructions, picks up the refrain by finishing George's sentences.

To George, this dream of having their own place means independence, security, being their own boss, and, most importantly, being "somebody." To Lennie, the dream is like the soft animals he pets: It means security, the responsibility of tending to the rabbits, and a sanctuary where he won't have to be afraid. To Candy, who sees the farm as a place where he can assert a responsibility he didn't take when he let Carlson kill his dog, it offers security for old age and a home where he will fit in. For Crooks, the little farm will be a place where he can have self-respect, acceptance, and security. For each man—George, Lennie, Candy, and Crooks—human dignity is an integral part of the dream.

Having and sharing the dream, however, are not enough to bring it to fruition. Each man must make a sacrifice or battle some other force that seeks, intentionally or not, to steal the dream away. Initially, the obstacles are difficult but not insurmountable: staying out of trouble, not spending money on liquor or in bordellos, and working at the ranch long enough to save the money for a down payment. But greater obstacles soon become apparent. Some of these obstacles are external (the threat from Curley's wife and Curley's violence, for example, as well as the societal prejudices that plague each man); others are internal (such as Lennie's strength and his need to touch soft things). For George, the greatest threat to the dream is Lennie himself; ironically, it is Lennie who also makes the dream worthwhile.

Loneliness

In addition to dreams, humans crave contact with others to give life meaning. Loneliness is present throughout this novel. On the most obvious level, we see this isolation when the ranch hands go into town on Saturday night to ease their loneliness with alcohol and women. Similarly, Lennie goes into Crook's room to find someone with whom to talk, and later Curley's wife comes for the same reason. Crooks says, "A guy goes nuts if he ain't got nobody. Don't make no difference who the guy is, long's he's with you." Even Slim mentions, "I seen the guys that go around on the ranches alone. That ain't no good. They don't have no fun. After a long time they get mean."

George's taking care of Lennie and the dream of the farm are attempts to break the pattern of loneliness that is part of the human condition. Similarly, Lennie's desire to pet soft things comes from his need to feel safe and secure, to touch something that gives him that feeling of not being alone in the world. For Lennie, the dream of the farm parallels that security.

George and Lennie, however, are not the only characters who struggle against loneliness. Although present in all the characters to some degree, the theme of loneliness is most notably present in Candy, Crooks, and Curley's wife. They all fight against their isolation in whatever way they can. Until its death, Candy's dog stopped Candy from being alone in the world. After its death, Candy struggles against loneliness by sharing in George and Lennie's dream. Curley's wife is also lonely; she is the only female on the ranch, and her husband has forbidden anyone to talk with her. She combats her loneliness by flirting with the ranch hands. Crooks is isolated because of his skin color. As the only black man on the ranch, he is not allowed into the bunkhouse with the others, and he does not associate with them. He combats his loneliness with books and his work, but even he realizes that these things are no substitute for human companionship.

Steinbeck reinforces the theme of loneliness in subtle and not so subtle ways. In the vicinity of the ranch, for example, is the town of Soledad. The town's name, not accidentally, means "solitude" or "alone." Also, the others' reactions to George and Lennie traveling together reinforces that, in Steinbeck's world, traveling with someone else is unusual. When George and Lennie arrive at the ranch, four other characters—the boss, Candy, Crooks, and Slim—all comment on the suspicious nature of two guys traveling together. This companionship seems strange and, according to at least the boss and Curley, the relationship is sexual or exploitative financially.

Barriers

Unfortunately, despite a need for companionship, people set up barriers that maintain loneliness, and they sustain those barriers by being inhumane to each other. One barrier is based on gender: The bunkhouse is a male world, where women are not to be trusted. While Curley's wife is always looking for attention, Curley's jealousy causes all the hands to stay away from her. Although Curley's wife is often portrayed as cruel and troublesome (and therefore, we can see why she is left alone), the real thing that isolates her is that she is a female in an all-male world. Race is another barrier. Crooks, for example, must occupy a room in the stable alone, and he is not welcome in the bunkhouse. For Candy, the barriers are age and handicap. He is afraid that, when he is too old to work, he will be thrown out on the ash heap, a victim of a society that does not value age and discriminates against handicaps.

Powerlessness

Steinbeck's characters are often the underdogs, and he shows compassion toward them throughout the body of his writings. Powerlessness takes many forms—intellectual, financial, societal—and Steinbeck touches on them all.

Although Lennie is physically strong and would therefore seem to represent someone of power, the only power Lennie possesses is physical. Because of his mental handicap and his child-like way of perceiving the world, he is powerless against his urges and the forces that assail him. For example, he knows what it is to be good, and he doesn't want to be bad, but he lacks the mental acuity that would help him understand and, therefore, avoid the dangers that unfold before him. Hence, he must rely on George to protect him. George, in this regard, is also powerless. Although he can instruct Lennie on what to do and not do, and although he perceives the danger posed by Curley's wife, he cannot be with Lennie every hour of every day and, therefore, cannot truly protect Lennie from himself. In the end, the only thing that George can do is protect Lennie from the others.

Another type of powerlessness is economic. Because the ranch hands are victims of a society where they cannot get ahead economically, they must struggle again and again. George and Lennie face overwhelming odds in trying to get together a mere $600 to buy their own land. But they are not the only ones who have shared the dream of owning land, nor the only ones who have difficulty securing the mean by which to do it. As Crooks explains, "I seen guys nearly crazy with loneliness for land, but ever' time a whorehouse or a blackjack game took what it takes." In other words, it is part of the human condition to always want instant gratification rather than save for tomorrow. As long as the men spend their money on the weekends, they will continue to be powerless. On the other hand, living lives of unremitting loneliness and harshness makes companionship—even for a weekend—alluring enough to overshadow a dream. Furthermore, the men are paid so little that it is difficult to save enough to make a dream come true.

Crooks represents another type of powerlessness. As the sole black man on the ranch, he is isolated from the others, and, in ways that the others are not, subject to their whim. This is never more apparent than when Curley's wife threatens to have him lynched. Despite his inherent dignity, Crooks shrinks into himself, essentially becoming invisible under her assault. The fact that she, another powerless person, wields such power over him demonstrates how defenseless he is in this society.

Fate

Life's unpredictable nature is another subject that defines the human condition. The title of the novel is taken from the poem of Robert Burns, "To a Mouse On Turning Her Up in Her Nest with a Plow," November, 1785. Burns wrote that "The best laid schemes o' mice and men / Gang aft a-gley [often go astray], / And lea'v us nought but grief and pain, / For promised joy."

Just when it appears that George and Lennie will get their farm, fate steps in. Lennie just happens to be in the barn burying his dead pup when Curley's wife comes in. In this case, fate is given a hand by Lennie's inability to control his strength and understand what to do. Nevertheless, often life seems unpredictable and full of overwhelming difficulties.

Christian, Classical, and Natural Influences

Many critics have compared *Of Mice and Men* to influences from John Milton's *Paradise Lost* and the Bible. And, indeed, many of the events of Steinbeck's novel parallel the biblical stories of the loss of paradise and Cain and Abel. Of particular relevance to *Of Mice and Men* is the question posed in the biblical story of Cain and Abel: Am I my brother's keeper? Also relevant is the story of Adam and Eve and their being cast out of Eden. Although a biblical story, this story is also the basis of John Milton's epic poem, *Paradise Lost*, which describes Lucifer's (Satan's) fall from heaven and the creation of hell, as well as Eve and Adam's fall from grace.

Steinbeck was influenced by the Arthurian legends as well, and the fellowship embodied in these tales also is relevant to *Of Mice and Men*. The loyalty and companionship, the love and trust shown between George and Lennie, are similar to the comradeship of the knights of the Arthurian tales. The knight's pledge to help those who are less fortunate and to defend the poor and powerless is also a motif apparent in *Of Mice and Men*. Additionally, the idea that nothing endures forever—especially perfection—reflects an Arthurian influence.

Throughout his novel Steinbeck uses nature to reflect the mood of the scenes and provide locations that reinforce themes. Steinbeck was a lover of nature, particularly the California countryside, and he uses nature in this story as both a place of sanctuary and also a reflection of foreboding.

Loss of Paradise

There are parallels between the biblical tale of Adam and Eve and the events that transpire in *Of Mice and Men*. Of particular interest are the nature of imperfect humans, the presence of temptation, and the consequences of doing, as Lennie would say, a "bad thing."

The story of Adam and Eve's fall from grace is a tale of how even our "best laid plans" go astray because of the imperfection of our humanity. Though mankind was created in God's image, man's reaction to temptation causes him to lose his way. Just as man is imperfect, so Lennie represents the flawed human appetite that makes the chance for Eden futile. His desire to touch soft things and his inability to foresee the results of his actions put him in a collision course with other human beings. While he sometimes realizes he has "done a bad thing," he often loses his way because of temptation. The girl in Weed and Curley's wife are both temptations that encouraged his curiosity and that he could not resist.

Curley's wife also has a part to play, as the serpent in the garden. She is temptation—a liar and a manipulator of men in order to get her way. She could also be compared to Eve. In the Garden of Eden, Eve is curious about the forbidden tree. She tempts Adam and manipulates him in order to get her way. Like Eve, Curley's wife is curious about Lennie. From the moment she realizes he is the "machine" that hurt her husband, she is attracted to his strength. When they talk in the barn, she invites him to touch her soft hair, not realizing the consequences. Her actions are innocent, but the consequences are vast. Just as Eve's actions caused mankind to be sent out of the perfect place, Curley's wife's actions tempt Lennie, whose subsequent actions cause him and the others to lose their dream of a little farm.

Also, because Adam and Eve were thrown out of Eden for disobeying God, mankind is forced to live a pattern of loneliness and wandering, having thrown away existence in Eden. Steinbeck reinforces this idea when George asks about the worker who used to inhabit his bunk and is told by Candy that he just left, saying, "'gimme my time' one night like any guy would." George takes his spot, bringing Lennie along, an action causing suspicion in the minds of others on the ranch. Guys don't travel together. Even Slim comments on their unusual companionship. In the end, with Lennie's death, George is once again sentenced to wander alone and to reflect on the loss of Lennie in his life.

My Brother's Keeper

In the story of Cain and his brother Abel, found in the fourth chapter of Genesis, Cain, an imperfect human and son of Adam and Eve, slew his brother out of jealousy. When God asked Cain where his brother was, Cain replied, "Am I my brother's keeper?" God knew Cain murdered his brother and sentenced Cain to walk the earth as a wanderer. When the loneliness was too much for Cain to bear, he begged God to kill him and put an end to it, but God forbade anyone to kill Cain because he must be punished for breaking God's law.

This story has many parallels in *Of Mice and Men*. The first parallel is the question of Cain, "Am I my brother's keeper?" Steinbeck essentially asks this same question in his other works such as *The Grapes of Wrath* or *East of Eden* when he wonders if mankind should go alone in the world or be responsible and helpful to others who are less fortunate. In the character of George, the answer seems to be the latter. George takes responsibility for Lennie, and Lennie depends on him. Furthermore, the noble characters—such as Slim—are those that recognize and honor this responsibility.

When George kills Lennie, he is sentenced to be like the other migrant hands, no longer traveling with someone he loves and no longer with goals or a dream of a different future. George is sentenced to the scenario described by Crooks when he told the others that no one ever gets their dreams. George will now wander from ranch to ranch, alone like the other migrant workers, and he will live the nightmare he described when he talked about his life without Lennie: no companion, no roots, no future.

The Ephemeral Nature of Life

Steinbeck was also influenced by the Arthurian legends. These tales reinforce the ideas that perfection cannot last and that nothing is permanent. In the stories of Camelot, the dream of the perfect place—similar to the Garden of Eden—is lost because of human weakness. Just as Camelot comes crumbling down because of the illicit love of Lancelot for the king's wife and the improper circumstances of Arthur's birth, so mankind is always subject to temptation. In Steinbeck's story, the dream of the little farm is lost because of Lennie's inability to control his strength or make decisions about how he uses it. His weakness is one of intellect and common sense. The dream of perfection—their little farm—will always elude George and Lennie because they are far from perfection.

In addition, the fellowship of the knights in that story contains a human element that the reader sees in the love and compassion of George for Lennie and the trust and loyalty of Lennie for George. George tells the others that he took Lennie along with him—almost like a puppy—after Lennie's Aunt Clara died. But George also gets Lennie his own pup and laughs at Lennie's delight, and he tells Lennie to defend himself against Curley. George explains to Slim that he felt bad when he played a joke on Lennie and he will not ever do that again just to feel superior. George's frustration in the end—when Lennie remembers so well everything George tells him—is a measure of George's love before he mercifully kills his friend. Furthermore, Lennie constantly watches and emulates George, copying his actions and attitudes. George says, "If I tol' him to walk over a cliff, over he'd go." Whatever George says, Lennie quickly does. Throughout the story, their relationship reflects the same fellowship as the Arthurian knights who pledged their love and loyalty to each other.

Nature

Steinbeck also uses nature images to reinforce his themes and to set the mood. In Chapter One, for example, before Lennie and George get to the ranch, George decides they will stay at the pond overnight. This pool is a place of primeval innocence, a sanctuary away from the world of humans. If Lennie gets in trouble, it is the place to which he should return. In this scene, nature is a place of safety, a haven from the troubles of the world.

When Lennie returns to the pond in the last scene, nature is not so tranquil. The sun has left the valley, and a heron captures and swallows a water snake "while its tail waved frantically." The wind now rushes and drives through the trees in gusts, and the dry leaves fall from the sycamore. Instead of a place of happiness, dream retelling, and fellowship—as it was at the beginning—the pond is now a place of loneliness, fear, and death. Here, nature reflects the mood of the human world. Steinbeck's thoughts on man's relationship to the land is a motif throughout his writing.

The words of the Swedish Academy in awarding Steinbeck the Nobel Prize for Literature recognized this close relationship between man and the land in Steinbeck's writing: "But in him [Steinbeck] we find the American temperament also in his great feeling for nature, for the tilled soil, the wasteland, the mountains, and the ocean coasts, all an inexhaustible source of inspiration to Steinbeck in the midst of, and beyond, the world of human beings."

Symbolism in *Of Mice and Men*

An allegory is a story that uses character types to represent specific ideas and create a universal message. In *Of Mice and Men*, Steinbeck uses his characters, locations, animal imagery, and a simple game of cards to demonstrate to his readers that most people dream about lives of great significance. But in reality, most humans' limitations keep these dreams from coming true, and in the long run, they are destined to experience common lives.

Characters

George and Lennie are the only two characters in the novel who are explained in any detail. The other characters are all "types," or people whom the reader might recognize as one of a certain group. Even the names of the characters, short and descriptive, say something about them. Lennie Small, for instance, is anything but small physically, and other characters seem to notice and comment on that. His brain is small and his ability to reason is small, but his body is huge and very powerful. Curley's wife has no name, indicating her powerless position on the ranch.

Each of the characters represents a kind of person in American society and often one that is a victim of discrimination. For example, Crooks represents a segment of American society that is discriminated against because of race; Curley's wife, because of gender; Candy, because of old age and physical handicap. Carlson is a perfect example of a selfish oaf, interested only in his creature comforts and oblivious to any one else's feelings. Slim is the consummate example of understanding and gentleness beneath a wise and experienced exterior. The pugnacious Curley is the little guy who loves to flaunt his power and status. Each of these minor characters impact, negatively or positively, Lennie and George's dream of having their own farm.

Locations

The pool described in the first paragraph of the novel is a place of sanctuary. Away from the world of humans, "the Salinas River drops in close to the hillside bank and runs deep and green. The water is warm too, for it has slipped twinkling over the yellow sands in the sunlight before reaching the narrow pool." Steinbeck goes on to describe the "strong and rocky" Gabilan Mountains and the "golden foothill slopes." A gentle breeze and fresh, green willow trees line the pool. In this place of sanctuary, George and Lennie enjoy one last night before going in to the ranch. Here there are no voices, no "scary things" for Lennie, no hurry, and no concerns about work.

But the pool represents another kind of sanctuary. George asks Lennie if he can remember this place, especially since it is on the river, an easy sign for Lennie to follow. George repeats several times his directions to Lennie: "Lennie—if you jus' happen to get in trouble like you always done before, I want you to come right here an' hide in the brush . . . till I come for you." This is the place where Lennie can come and George can meet him and help him again as he did when Lennie got in trouble in Weed. If necessary, the pool will be their meeting place so they can get away once again. Later, when the doomed Lennie returns to the pool, he sadly repeats, "I di'n't forget, you bet. God damn. Hide in the brush an' wait for George." For Lennie, this is where George will make everything right, and he will be safe.

While this is also the place where Lennie's dream will die, it will do so with peace and tranquility, at least in Lennie's mind. When George describes the dream, later at this pool, the atmosphere of nature and its beauty obviously inspire his words. He tells Lennie, "You . . . an' me. Ever'body gonna be nice to you. Ain't gonna be no more trouble. Nobody gonna hurt nobody nor steal from 'em." Now this place has also become enmeshed in the retelling of the dream that will bring them better lives. And even though we know that the dream is retold here with another meaning for George, we also see that Lennie hears the story once again with eagerness in his voice and anticipation in his words. Here, in this beautiful place, George will save Lennie from the cruelty of Curley and help him die with his picture of their farm in his head.

The dream farm is another location; it does not exist in reality but is very real in the minds of Lennie and, eventually, George. It becomes a symbol for their relationship, and the retelling of the dream has become a ritual. This is the place where George and Lennie will have self-respect and independence. They will live off the fat of the land, and no one will tell them what to do. Lennie can have what he likes the best—soft rabbits to pet—and he will feel safe. George can have a more normal life that involves putting down roots and staying in one place. At the farm, George will also have an easier time keeping track of Lennie. When Candy offers the money to put down a payment, the symbol begins to become a reality. Unfortunately, the dream is an enchanted concept, and once its reality becomes possible, it begins to die.

In opposition to these two positive symbols is the bunkhouse, which represents the cruel world of reality. Even Lennie, with his mental handicap, can intuitively feel that the bunkhouse is not a good place. After meeting Curley, Lennie tells George, "I don't like this place, George. This ain't no good place. I wanna get outa here." And as soon as Curley's wife comes alone to the bunkhouse, George knows exactly where the trouble is going to originate. He cautions Lennie not to talk to Curley's wife and to stay away from Curley. It is also in the bunkhouse that we see discrimination (against Candy and Crooks), cruelty (Curley's wife's attack on Crooks and Curley's attack on Lennie), insensitivity (Carlson's killing Candy's dog), and suspicion (Curley's jealousy, several characters presumptions about why Lennie and George are traveling together). This is also a world in which fate often plays a hand, and the humans are frequently defenseless and see their "best laid plans" go awry.

Animal Imagery

Steinbeck also uses animal images in his story. Most often applied to Lennie, imagery is particularly apparent in his physical description. His hands are called "paws" and indicate trouble when he uses them. He lumbers along like a bear in Steinbeck's earliest descriptions of him. Lennie is also associated with rabbits, which are part of his dream (he will get to tend them on the farm) and because they are soft things he likes to pet. Rabbits also symbolize his realization that he is in trouble; if Lennie does "a bad thing," George will not let him tend the rabbits. In the last scene, when Lennie is at the pool, waiting for George, a rabbit appears to him, berating him and telling him that George will not let him care for the rabbits. In addition, Lennie's loyalty to George is frequently described like that of a dog, especially a terrier. Steinbeck chose these images because they connote particular traits: unleashed power, conscience, and loyalty. In this way, it helps the reader understand Lennie and why he often acts instinctively.

George's Card Game

Steinbeck is often described by critics as a believer in a "non-teleological world." This is a world where chance plays a major role. It is chance, for instance, that Slim happens to be in the barn when Curley comes into the bunkhouse looking for his wife. It is also chance that George is absent from the barn when Lennie is burying his pup and Curley's wife comes in. Steinbeck tries to show that man cannot understand everything that happens, nor can he control the world around him. For this reason, events often appear to be random.

George's Solitaire game in the bunkhouse is exactly that. It symbolizes the random appearance of events just as cards are drawn out at random from the deck. All is a matter of chance in Solitaire, and the same is true of the events in the book that Steinbeck thought about titling "Something That Happened." The isolation of the ranch and the interplay of personalities in the bunkhouse also contribute to the idea of chance. The world is unpredictable, and in this setting, plans often "go awry."

Hands

Hands are also used symbolically throughout the novel. The men on the ranch are called "hands," indicating that each has a job to do to make the ranch work as a whole. This takes away their humanity and individual personalities. They are workers, not men. Lennie's hands, or paws, are symbols of trouble. Whenever he uses them—as he does on Curley—trouble ensues. Candy's missing hand is a symbol of his helplessness in the face of advancing old age and his fear that he will be deemed useless and fired when only one hand is not enough. George's hands are small and strong, the hands of a doer and planner. Curley's hands are mean and cruel and one, of course, is crushed in the machine that is Lennie; Curley's hand that he keeps soft for his wife is a symbol of his impotence and inability to satisfy his wife sexually. Crooks' hands are pink, and Curley's wife's hands have red nails. Slim has large, skillful hands like those of "a temple dancer." The hand images represent the essence of each person.

CliffsNotes Review

Use this CliffsNotes Review to test your understanding of the original text and reinforce what you've learned in this book. After you work through the review and essay questions, identify the quote section, and the fun and useful practice projects, you're well on your way to understanding a comprehensive and meaningful interpretation of *Of Mice and Men*.

Q&A

1. Early in the novel when Lennie likes to pet soft things, Steinbeck is using what technique?

   a. symbolism

   b. foreshadowing

   c. figurative language

2. Candy described Curley's new wife as a

   a. tart

   b. good cook

   c. complainer

3. George and Lennie's plan for a farm draws the interest of

   a. Curley and his wife

   b. Slim and Candy

   c. Candy and Crooks

4. "You done it, di'n't you? I s'pose you're glad. Ever'body knowed you'd mess things up. You wasn't no good." This is said

   a. by Lennie to his dead pup

   b. by George to Lennie in the barn

   c. by Candy to Curley's dead wife

5. George kills Lennie because

   a. Lennie was guilty of murder

   b. A long court trial would be hard on Lennie

   c. George was afraid Curley would hurt Lennie

   Answers: (1) b. (2) a. (3) c. (4) c. (5) c.

Identify the Quote

1. A guy goes nuts if he ain't got nobody. Don't make no difference who the guy is, long's he's with you. I tell ya a guy gets too lonely an' he gets sick.

2. When I think of the swell time I could have without you, I go nuts. I never get no peace.

3. When they had them previews I coulda went to them, an' spoke in the radio, and it wouldn'ta cost me a cent because I was in the pitcher.

4. You seen what they done to my dog tonight? They says he wasn't no good to himself nor nobody else. When they can me here I wisht somebody'd shoot me.

> **Answers:** (1) [Crooks, when he is talking to Lennie in his room about how lonely he is.] (2) [George, explaining to Lennie how he is too big a burden for George.] (3) [Curley's wife, explaining to Lennie about the dreams she had before she married Curley.] (4) [Candy, describing his fear that he will be turned out because of his age and handicap.]

Essay Questions

1. Steinbeck was going to name his story "Something That Happened." Instead, he named if *Of Mice and Men.* Which title do you think is more appropriate to the novel as a whole? Explain your answer.

2. In tragedies, the central character comes to a realization about his life or an understanding of life in general as a result of his suffering. Is this true of *Of Mice and Men*? Explain.

3. Explain Steinbeck's use of foreshadowing in *Of Mice and Men.*

4. Choose a symbol used by Steinbeck and explain its significance in the novel.

Practice Projects

1. Research migrant workers in America during the 1930s, today, or both. Give a presentation to the class detailing what you find. Note any similarities or differences between what you discovered in your research and Steinbeck's portrayal in *Of Mice and Men.*

2. Interview three people who lived during the Depression and present your findings to the class.

3. Watch at least one film version of the novel and compare it with the book.

CliffsNotes Resource Center

The learning doesn't need to stop here. CliffsNotes Resource Center shows you the best of the best— links to the best information in print and online about the author and/or related works. And don't think that this is all we've prepared for you; we've put all kinds of pertinent information at www. cliffsnotes.com. Look for all the terrific resources at your favorite bookstore or local library and on the Internet. When you're online, make your first stop www.cliffsnotes.com where you'll find more incredibly useful information about *Of Mice and Men*.

Books

This CliffsNotes book provides a meaningful interpretation of *Of Mice and Men*. If you are looking for information about the author and/or related works, check out these other publications:

John Steinbeck, by Warren French, is a series of chapters on Steinbeck's life and works. Chapter 7 deals with *Of Mice and Men*. The book also includes a bibliography of critical works. New York: Twayne Publishers, 1961.

Steinbeck: The Man and His Work, by Richard Astro and Tetsumaro Hayashi, contains a collection of essays given as papers in 1971 by members of the John Steinbeck Society. Each paper is on a different aspect of Steinbeck and his works. Corvallis, Ore: Oregon State University Press, 1971.

The Wide World of John Steinbeck, by Peter Lisca, is one of the most famous books on Steinbeck. It contains chapters on all of his works prior to 1958. New Brunswick, N.J.: Rutgers University Press, 1958.

Steinbeck: A Life in Letters, by Elaine Steinbeck and Robert Wallsten, is a collection of Steinbeck's extensive correspondence that provide insights into his thinking. New York: Viking, 1975.

Steinbeck and His Critics, A Record of Twenty-Five Years, edited by E.W. Tedlock, Jr., and C.W. Wicker, contains critical essays by Steinbeck on his own writing and also essays by seventeen other writers. Albuquerque: University of New Mexico Press, 1957.

The Short Novels of John Steinbeck, edited by Jackson J. Benson, contains an essay by Anne Loftis, "A Historical Introduction to *Of Mice and Men*," that explores the historical context of the novel in 1930s California. Durham: Duke University Press, 1990.

***Readings on Of* Mice and Men**, edited by Bruno Leone, contains nineteen essays on themes, symbols, structure, criticism, and the play of the novel. It also offers a bibliography and chronology of works. Part of the Greenhaven Press Literary Companion to American Literature Series, San Diego, CA: Greenhaven Press, 1998.

It's easy to find books published by Wiley Publishing, Inc. You'll find them in your favorite bookstores (on the Internet and at a store near you). We also have three Web sites that you can use to read about all the books we publish:

- www.cliffsnotes.com

- www.dummies.com

- www.wiley.com

Internet

Check out these Web resources for more information about John Steinbeck and *Of Mice and Men*:

Center for Steinbeck Studies at San Jose State University, www.sjsu.edu/depts/steinbec/srchome.html—This site contains Steinbeck's life and works, archives, Web site links, and his Nobel Prize speech.

National Steinbeck Center, www.steinbeck.org/index2.html—This site has information on Steinbeck's life, works, facts, and other links.

Steinbeck's California Novels, www.ac.wwu.edu/~stephan/Steinbeck/—This site offers maps with the geographical locations of *Of Mice and Men*, a brief summary of the novel, and a character list.

Extensive California Site, http://tlc.ai.org/Steinbec.htm—This site includes a guide to Monterey County, a set of teacher's lesson plans on the novel, biographical sites, newspaper articles, a movie database, photographs, sites related to both Steinbeck's life and the works, sites on geography, and specific sites for *Of Mice and Men*.

Next time you're on the Internet, don't forget to drop by www. cliffsnotes.com. We created an online Resource Center that you can use today, tomorrow, and beyond.

Films and Other Recordings

Following are some film adaptations of *Of Mice and Men*:

Of Mice and Men, MGM, 1992. Directed by and starring Gary Sinise as George and John Malkovich as Lennie, this film is very faithful to the novel and received positive reviews from critics. It is available on video.

Of Mice and Men, Metromedia Productions, 1981. Directed by Reza Badiyi and starring Robert Blake as George and Randy Quaid as Lennie, this is a good adaptation with some added scenes and material; sound track is pure Americana and reinforces Steinbeck's love of the land. Available on video.

Of Mice and Men, Hal Roach Studios, Inc., 1939. Directed by Lewis Milestone and starring Burgess Meredith as George and Lon Chaney, Jr., as Lennie, this film was nominated for four Academy Awards, including best picture. Available on video.

Magazines and Journals

For more information on *Of Mice and Men* and Steinbeck's work, consult the following articles:

Shurgot, Michael W. "A Game of Cards in Steinbeck's *Of Mice and Men*," Steinbeck Quarterly, Winter-Spring 1982: 38–43. Shurgot discusses three symbolic interpretations of George's game of solitaire in *Of Mice and Men*.

Spilka, Mark. "Of George and Lennie and Curley's Wife: Sweet Violence in Steinbeck's Eden," Modern Fiction Studies, 1974: 169–179. Spilka analyzes gender and sexuality in these three characters from the novel.

Goldhurst, William. "*Of Mice and Men*: John Steinbeck's Parable of the Curse of Cain," Western American Literature, Summer 1971: 126–128. Contains a discussion of the Cain and Abel themes of the novel.

Send Us Your Favorite Tips

In your quest for knowledge, have you ever experienced that sublime moment when you figure out a trick that saves time or trouble? Perhaps you realized you were taking ten steps to accomplish something that could have taken two. Or you found a little-known workaround that achieved great results. If you've discovered a useful resource that gave you insight into or helped you understand *Of Mice and Men* and you'd like to share it, the CliffsNotes staff would love to hear from you. Go to our Web site at www.cliffsnotes.com and click the Talk to Us button. If we select your tip, we may publish it as part of CliffsNotes Daily, our exciting, free e-mail newsletter. To find out more or to subscribe to a newsletter, go to www.cliffsnotes.com on the Web.

Index

(continued)